Cathedral Cats

Also available from Collins by Richard Surman

Church Cats

Cathedral Cats

Richard Surman

Collins

Collins
a division of HarperCollins Publishers
77–85 Fulham Palace Road, London W6 8JB
www.collins.co.uk

First published in Great Britain in 2005 by
HarperCollins Publishers

10 9 8 7 6 5 4 3 2

A catalogue record for this book is available from the British
Library.

ISBN 0 00 718280 5

Colour Reproduction by Dot Gradations Ltd, UK
Printed and bound in Hong Kong by
Printing Express

Collins

Contents

Introduction

'A man has to work so hard so that something of his personality stays alive. A tomcat has it so easy, he has only to spray and his presence is there for years on rainy days'

Albert Einstein

I'm not shy about my enduring admiration for cats. I grew up with them, and carry the scars to prove it. I regularly perform the supreme and nauseating sacrifice of opening tinned cat food at six o'clock in the morning. They share my office, every nook and cranny of our home. They dig their claws into my shins as a sign of pure pleasure, and magically become a deadweight on my lap whenever I want to move.

So what do I get in return? Good conversation, and (mostly) uncontentious company. No one will ever convince me that my own two Burmese cats don't talk to me, and it's not just about food either: the weather, politics, art; you name it, my cats have an opinion. Cats are the most fascinating, enchanting,

exasperating and contrary of all nature's creatures. They do not substitute for human relationships, they complement them.

The cats portrayed in this new collection of *Cathedral Cats* cover the whole gamut, ranging from farm cats like Lichfield Cathedral's Kim, to aristocrats such as Durham Cathedral's Olsen and Hansen. But no matter what the lineage of each cat is, they all have these essential feline features in common: a flagrant disregard for rules and convention; an uncanny tendency to identify and do exactly the opposite of what is wanted; an innate belief in their right to go anywhere they want; an ability to soothe and lower one's blood pressure; and astonishing grace and dexterity. It would be fanciful and romantic to imagine that in past times cats were welcomed into cathedrals for any reason other than their skills at keeping down vermin, but today the number of cathedrals that good-humouredly tolerate the presence of cats is impressive. Maybe it has to do with the type of person that lives and works in today's cathedrals: independent, and perhaps slightly idiosyncratic – the ideal companion for such independent and idiosyncratic animals.

As for the cathedrals, they are a strange combination of the magnificent and the everyday. On one hand there are the awe-inspiring architecture and settings of these great buildings, while on the other hand there are all the human elements that have brought about these monolithic expressions of faith and power. Even the grandest cathedral has its human aspect, in the lives of those who live and work in it, and in its history and construction. Imagine the pride and flourish with which, for example, the travelling masons engraved their marks at Southwell Minster, the apprehension with which a master mason knocked away the supports under a new arch, or the head-scratching of the monastic builders as they proceeded by trial and error to create such complex, beautiful buildings.

All these people were pioneers in their own fields. Then there were the towers: what a mind-boggling history of catastrophe and reconstruction. In times

LEFT
Steve Mellor in conversation with Wolfie
ABOVE
Leofric, featured in Country Living

gone by, towers were built on the assumption that if one fell down, another could always be erected in its place. And fall down they did, regularly and spectacularly!

There are whimsical things too, like the games scratched into the stonework by young novices in the cloisters of Gloucester Cathedral (I assume it was the young novices, and not some particularly bored senior monks), and the mischievous depictions of people and animals in misericords and corbels; for an eccentric solution to a practical problem, look no further than the mechanical conducting hand in the organ loft of Ripon Cathedral. Through the centuries these great buildings have reflected changes in the surrounding world: they carry with them the stories of thousands of ordinary people, they bear historical witness to endeavour, tyranny, intolerance and reconciliation, and still the cathedrals remain places of worship, inspiration and peace for anyone prepared to take a moment away from the turmoil of modern life.

Many people helped me find a new line up of cathedral cats. In particular, I'd like to thank Pauline Hawkins at Lichfield Cathedral, Catherine Spender, Simon Lole and Alun Williams at Salisbury Cathedral, Tom Morton at Portsmouth Cathedral, Angela Prior at Canterbury Cathedral, Fiona Barnaby and Nicholas Fry at Chester Cathedral, Penelope Utting at Chichester Cathedral, Alison Chambers at Hereford Cathedral, Rosemary Murgatroyd at Ripon Cathedral, Sarah Friswell at St Edmundsbury Cathedral, Anna Davidson at St Mary's Episcopal Cathedral, Jackie Pope and Joanne Green at Westminster Abbey, Fiona Price at Gloucester Cathedral, Susie Arnold at Worcester Cathedral, Chris Stone at Rochester Cathedral and Stephen Wickner at Ely Cathedral. I'm also very grateful to Adam Munthe for providing me with a suitably eccentric and secluded hideaway in which to write, and of course to Ian Metcalfe at Collins for providing me with the opportunity to tackle anew a cherished topic, *Cathedral Cats*.

For my children and grandchildren

Daisy and Lazarus
St Edmundsbury

'The cat, which is a solitary beast, is single minded and goes its way alone; but the dog, like his master, is confused in his mind'
H.G. Wells

With a home that borders leafy abbey churchyard grounds, a ruined castle and a large cathedral, Daisy and Lazarus have one of the most extensive territories of all the cats in this book. And for a cat named Lazarus, what more suitable territory than a graveyard! Catherine Todd, Rector of the Horringe Benefices, her husband Andrew, Residentiary Canon at St Edmundsbury Cathedral, and their three children, Benedict, Hannah and Lydia, live in a Georgian house that fronts on to the main road. Bury St Edmunds is a busy town, so the world outside the front door is a no-go zone for the cats. Fortunately for Daisy and Lazarus, the back of the house gives onto safer territory. It overlooks the delightful tree-lined promenades and crumbling gravestones of the old

THE CATHEDRAL

Unlike many of Britain's cathedrals, the final shapes of which were more or less determined in the middle ages, St Edmundsbury has acquired its present appearance since the 18th century, with its most striking new feature, the central lantern tower, only recently completed.

Little of the substance of the original Benedictine Abbey of St Edmund remains, but there are some interesting remnants – the rebuilt abbey gatehouse, the excavated footings of the eastern end of the abbey, and the curious site of houses incorporated into the ruined western end of the abbey church. The present cathedral is half the length of the old abbey, which gives a pretty good idea of the scale of the original monastic buildings.

Most recently, the choir and crossing were redesigned to accommodate the requirements of cathedral services, and the lantern tower has now been completed, thanks to a generous bequest, Millennium funding and public appeals.

abbey churchyard, and enjoys a fine view of the entire length of the cathedral, complete with its magnificent new crossing tower. I was curious to know how far the cats roamed within this vast area, and Catherine thought that they went no further than the old abbey church. But I saw Lazarus nipping around the east end of the cathedral and heading for the knot garden and castle with the determination of someone who knows exactly where he's going.

The family's previous cats were called Archie and Mehitabel. This is a family with a penchant for eccentric names – a cat named after a literary cockroach, one rat called Edward, Frodo the hamster, Malteser the guinea pig, and last but not least two rabbits, Sirius and Merlin. There are gerbils too: I didn't note their names, but they're probably Gandalf and Einstein. Daisy shows great concern for the well-being of the gerbils, sitting watching them intently for hours on end; one day she tried to help them escape by destroying the cage. But despite protesting the purity of her intentions, it was decided that the gerbils would be better off in a room to which Daisy has no access.

The cats came from different litters of British Short-hairs. Lazarus was a weak kitten, who had been abandoned, and the breeder placed him in the same litter as Daisy to see if he would revive, which he did – and received his name in tribute to the unexpected recovery. My brief observations of both cats don't entirely align with those of the family. I was told that

Daisy is more adventurous than Lazarus, but it was Lazarus that was slinking along the side of the cathedral, Lazarus who stalked off confidently in the direction of the knot garden and ruined castle; Daisy was just rolling around on an old gravestone and hiding under a neighbour's car. Maybe they act differently in front of a camera, but you can never be quite sure what is in the mind of a cat: Adlai Stevenson once said that 'it is in the nature of cats to do a certain amount of unescorted roaming,' and I

PREVIOUS PAGE
Lazarus: a passion for brown bread
ABOVE
The graveyard is Lazarus's favourite playground
OPPOSITE
Daisy, lurking by the cathedral

think that Lazarus does a lot more of it than his family is aware of.

The two cats live together in a state of entente demi-cordiale. They'll occupy the same room, pass relatively close to each other – and that's as far as it goes. Lazarus will insist on having the occasional tussle with Daisy; no one is sure why, as he always comes off worse. With this relationship of grudging tolerance in place, both cats generally go their separate ways. The whole site, originally the Benedictine abbey of St Edmund, contained an abbey church twice the length of the present cathedral, as well as fishponds, breweries, workshops and granaries.

The gardens and riverside meadows are a popular place for picnics, but the two cats have not yet worked out the tourist potential for acting as a team. Maybe neither has the need, as Daisy has found out that chapter meetings can be pretty productive, especially in other people's houses, where she can anticipate a variety of menus. For his part, Lazarus has developed some very strange food habits, principal among which is a passion for granary bread. Picture a cat confronted with a bird table on which there are several plump birds. Then imagine a cat leaping out of cover onto the table: mayhem should ensue. In Lazarus's case it does, insofar as he doesn't employ stealth. Rather than being a meat-seeking missile, Lazarus is a bread-gobbling blunderer. The element of surprise is only necessary if one's prey can move. Lazarus only wants the bread on the bird table, so he'll scramble up, taking no care to conceal his approach whatsoever. This obsession with bread goes further. He will take a loaf out of the hand: he'll sit by the bread bin and mew appealingly, patiently waiting. And if the bread is sliced and in a packet – no problem. Lazarus patiently picks at the wrapping, then carefully claws out one (or two) slices.

Both cats have followed the construction of the new cathedral tower, from the shelter of the ruined western end of the old abbey church. The scaffolding has provided limitless opportunities for Daisy to view her kingdom while Lazarus, unimpressed by her acrobatic feats, is more interested in finding a friendly baker.

Rhubarb, Fungus and Magic
Canterbury Cathedral

'One cat just leads to another'

Ernest Hemingway

There is a cacophony of cats at Canterbury Cathedral – choir cats, school cats, canonical cats and visiting cats. Such a vigorous feline population is hardly out of character for a place that has always been a hive of activity; down the centuries Canterbury Cathedral has thrived on the visits of pilgrims thronging to the shrine of St Thomas à Becket, and tourists come to see the tombs of Henry VI, his wife Joan of Navarre, and Edward the Black Prince.

Adjacent to the Great Cloisters (through which legend has it that Thomas à Becket fled from his pursuers), in a house that forms part of a medieval gateway, live two cats, Rhubarb and Fungus – mother and daughter. The household in which they live is best described as an

THE CATHEDRAL

Canterbury's imposing cathedral almost overpowers the city that surrounds it, in physical terms and also in the weight of its history which has secured its status as a UNESCO World Heritage site.

There are many striking views of and near the cathedral, not least that of the spectacular sixteenth century Christchurch Gate, which opens onto the cathedral precincts. The original cathedral, built by St Augustine, was destroyed in a fire in 1067, and again fire destroyed much of its Norman replacement, although the shrine of St Thomas à Becket, located in the crypt, was spared. Thousands of pilgrims came to venerate the saint, and as the centuries passed there came visitors also to the tombs of Henry VI and his wife Joan of Navarre, and of Edward, the Black Prince – all of whose tombs survived the Reformation, unlike St Thomas's, which was destroyed by Cromwell's troops. Today Canterbury Cathedral remains not just a tourist destination but a place of pilgimage and a worldwide symbol for Christianity.

ecclesiastical ark, and presiding over this melange of peaceful chaos are Canon Edward Condry, Canon Treasurer at the cathedral, and his wife Sarah.

Before moving to Canterbury, the Condry family lived in the Northamptonshire countryside. Sarah Condry comes from a farming family, which might go some way towards explaining why they had hens, a rooster, guinea pigs, cat, dogs, Russian hamsters and salamanders. And like any other conventional ecclesiastical family, they had a pony and trap, of course.

The four children, Fran, Felix, Jerome and Hannah, are nominally responsible for regulating the animal affairs of the household. Take the duck for instance: a well-meaning vet friend of the family gives Hannah stray ducks to take home. Ducks need water to swim in, which Hannah provides by running regular baths; this plays havoc with the water bills because the duck keeps diving down and pulling the plug out. Fungus and Rhubarb do not like the duck; on passing the bathroom door and hearing ecstatic quacking and the slapping of happy wings on water, they exchange nervous glances and high tail it out of the house.

As members of such a varied household, both cats have had to make major adjustments to their natural inclinations; Fungus, when really pressed for somewhere peaceful quiet and warm to lay her head, pulls up the lid on Little Nell's cage, clambers in and snuggles up to her (Little Nell is a guinea pig). As for the dogs of the house – Jumble, Tigger and Jim – the cats will sometimes use them as scratching posts, but for the most part, they are ignored. This psychological approach has not been entirely successful: cats can cope with being ignored, but an ignored dog just tries harder and harder to attract attention. For an intent cat, there is nothing worse than a dog nosing in, butting the cat for attention and whacking its tail loudly against a nearby dustbin. Rhubarb wasn't that interested in her kitten, Fungus, when she was born, but in the face of pressure from the other species with which they were forced to share their home environment, mother and daughter closed ranks, and

have been inseparable ever since. They have learned to cope with the blundering friendliness of the family dogs, the hissing of the salamander, duck fostering and the attentions of a giant rabbit, and have been steadfast in the face of attacks by the choir cats. If life gets a bit hectic they wander together over to the cloisters, where they charm the occasional edible treat from cathedral visitors. Occasionally their timing is out, and they come nose to nose with Magic, another cathedral cat at Canterbury.

Magic also likes the cloisters. She goes there regularly, and when she finds Fungus and Rhubarb there also,

PREVIOUS PAGE
Rhubarb and Fungus, trying unsuccessfully to ignore Tigger the dog
LEFT
Magic: unmusical encounters with Fungus and Rhubarb in the cloisters
RIGHT
Rhubarb keeps a wary eye on the cloisters

Not even the dogs can follow Fungus
out of the window

Magic's magical view of the cathedral

the cloisters echo to distinctly unholy sounds; it's a bit like buskers competing for space. Magic lived in the Condry's old house before moving to another part of the cathedral precincts with her family, the Rev. Dr Canon Richard Marsh, his wife Elizabeth, and their daughter Phoebe. Magic is very much Phoebe's cat, and when Phoebe is practising music (singing and contrabassoon) will sit resignedly, ignoring the occasional fluffed note.

Like Fungus and Rhubarb, Magic has also had to cope with dogs, and a couple of snakes too. The Marsh family previously lived at Lambeth Palace, where Phoebe had two snakes – Bishop and Archie – as well as a feisty border collie called Benedict. Magic, like Rochester's Figaro, learned to live with the snakes because, well, there was no alternative. But Benedict the border collie was succeeded, to Magic's dismay, by Benedict the black labrador. He and Magic don't really hit it off that well; the relationship between the two is one of frosty stand-offishness.

On arrival at Canterbury, Magic had to work to establish her new territory. And even after word got out that there was a new cat around, she still had annoyances. Walking through the study one day, a slight movement caught her eye; under the desk was a very embarrassed cat, trying to make itself as unobstrusive as possible. The situation was noisily resolved – leading to indignant talk amongst the cats of Canterbury Cathedral about the need for tolerance.

In fact the King's School's headmaster's cat came to remonstrate with Magic, but to no avail. Magic didn't give an inch: she loves her new house at the cathedral. At the end of a large private garden are the old city walls, on which she sits, watching the outside world scurry by. At the other end, the Bell Harry Tower rises majestically over the cathedral nave, in front of which can be seen the Corona chapel, the original home of St Thomas à Becket's relics.

Visits to the deanery are a regular item in her diary, although one day she had to explain indignantly – and ultimately unconvincingly – that she was only looking at the whole salmon laid out for lunch. And unlike Rhubarb and Fungus, Magic has found her way into the cathedral, another regular part of her perambulations around her precinct. The Good Friday services perplexed her a little: they are very long, so she distracted herself (and much of the congregation) by hopping on and off the canons' stalls, eventually settling with a sigh of resignation to an extended grooming session. She enjoys being with the choir too: this seems to be favourite pastime for cathedral cats, and Magic has stolen the show more than once! But on a quiet summer's evening, with the cathedral almost entirely to herself, Magic likes nothing more than to stretch out on the throne of St Augustine, having a good wash while she plans the next day's itinerary.

Tomkins
Chelmsford Cathedral

'Most of us rather like our cats to have a streak of wickedness. I should not feel quite easy in the company of any cat that walked about the house with a saintly expression'
Beverley Nichols

An important part of the welcome given to visitors of the new Cathedral Centre of Chelmsford Cathedral is provided by Tomkins, a splendid, portly black and white cat named after the Elizabethan composer Thomas Tomkins, and owned by Peter Nardone, organist and Director of Music at Chelmsford Cathedral.

Tomkins is a rescue cat in every sense. When first found, he was in the garden of a derelict house in South London, frantically struggling to rid himself of a kitten collar, not because he disliked collars on principle, but because he was two years old, and the collar around his neck was for a six-month kitten: it was slowly strangling him. The fact that Tomkins had

THE CATHEDRAL

One of the smallest cathedrals in England, Chelmsford Cathedral serves the second largest diocese, with a population of over two and half million, covering some 600 parishes, as well as the suburban boroughs of East London.

Bishop Maurice – Lord of the Manor of Chelmsford – inspired the bridging of the river Chelmer, and as a result of the regular flow of traffic between London and Colchester, a thriving settlement sprang up, and with it the parish church of St Mary. Rebuilt in the fifteenth century, the church finally became a cathedral in 1914.

The arms of the most famous president of the United States are displayed in the South Porch (his great-great-grandfather was a rector in Essex), and the South Porch was enhanced in the early 1950s as a tribute to the endeavours of American air crews based in the area during the Second World War.

PREVIOUS PAGE
Tomkins on parade
ABOVE
There's a softer side to Tomkins, not often seen by the neighbourhood cats
RIGHT
Tomkins and Saint Francis of Assissi – an act of phoney contrition

survived at all was a tribute to his strength and determination. Relieved of the collar, Tomkins was transformed into a character brimming over with gratitude and confidence, and through the efforts of the Cats Protection League, was introduced to Peter Nardone. Tomkins was Peter's first cat (and Peter probably Tomkins' first consistent human contact) and he rewarded Peter's kindness with the kind of devotion more commonly expected of dogs. When Peter moved to his current position at Chelmsford Cathedral, he and Tomkins took up residence in a secluded house on the edge of the cathedral gardens, separated from the cathedral by the recently built Cathedral Centre, and a busy road – which Tomkins has the good sense not to cross. The cathedral is a modest but airy and pleasing gothic building, whose external walls show the distinctive use of flint rubble and inlay typical of East Anglian church construction. Although one of the smallest English cathedrals, it serves the second largest diocese, with a population of over two and a half million, covering six hundred parishes: it is noted for its vibrant parish life and music, as well as being the venue for a renowned annual music and arts festival.

When Tomkins first arrived, he was delighted to discover that beyond his small fenced garden were two acres of sprawling lawns, overhung with trees, and criss-crossed with winding paths leading through dense shrubbery to the Cathedral Centre. Not only did he have a loving home, but an enormous garden all to

himself. There was one drawback: the legions of Chelmsford cats – who thought that the Cathedral Centre gardens belonged to them – had not been informed of Tomkins' impending arrival, nor were they willing to recognise his claim to the territory. It didn't take long for Tomkins to realize that he had to sort out this undisciplined rabble. Having spent the first two years of his life on the streets of Peckham in South London, it was the kind of problem that Tomkins was used to, and within a week the area was cleared. The Chelmsford cats now avoid this garden as carefully as people avoid quicksand; mother cats terrify their kittens with tales of a ghostly black and white cat that explodes out of nowhere. Even dogs twitch, nervously, as they walk by.

In a secluded grotto in the gardens stands a statue of St Francis of Assissi (patron saint of all animals), to which Tomkins started to pay regular visits; so much so that Peter was moved to wonder if Tomkins was suffering from overwhelming attacks of conscience arising from his perhaps over-vigorous garden cleansing. Others, more cynical than Peter, speculated that in the cause of good public relations, Tomkins had decided that devout postures might serve as a diversion from his enthusiastic policing of the gardens. Whatever the explanation, Peter worries that over time the expression on the saint's face seems to have become slightly less benign, more exasperated, almost disapproving – but maybe it's just a trick of the light. If all this gives the impression that Tomkins is a

formidable cat, then the balance must be redressed. His outside life is not entirely composed of border patrols and dawn raids: Tomkins habitually calls in at the deanery, where there is always a comfortable armchair at his disposal. And when he's up that way, Tomkins invariably stops at the cathedral music offices to see Christine Hall, Peter Nardone's assistant. Around the time of the lively annual festival, Tomkins entertains and is entertained by the artists, performers, international musicians and groups who pass through here. Tomkins also diverts the many visitors from North America who come to Chelmsford; the South Porch was enhanced in the 1950s as a tribute to the endeavours and sacrifices of USAF air crews based in the area during the Second World War. George Washington's arms are also on display in the South Porch (his great-great-grandfather was a rector in Essex.) And if the choristers happen to be en route from the cathedral, he happily brings up the rear, rather like a sheep cat.

But for all his adventurings outside the home, inside it Tomkins leads a tranquil existence: every day he goes, tail lifted in greeting, to meet the postman. He always calls when the newspapers come through the letter box (though this may have more to do with his habit of sleeping on the doormat than a deliberate policy of helpfulness).

There is one area of dissonance in all this domestic harmony – the piano. Tomkins may bear the name of a composer, but it doesn't follow that he likes music, and in the early days the sound of the piano being played was enough to drive Tomkins to drink (milk laced with brandy, please). Early attempts on his part to prevent Peter playing the piano failed dismally. No amount of wailing, leaping onto Peter's lap or attacking the hammers inside the piano could deter Peter from

playing, and in the end Tomkins just fled. These days he is a little more prepared for musical onslaughts: at the sound of the grand piano being opened, Tomkins makes his way hastily upstairs to the guest bedroom, clambers onto the bed and sticks his head under a pillow.

Olsen and Hansen
Chester Cathedral

'There are two means of refuge from the miseries of life: music and cats'
Albert Schweitzer

The first sign of the cats in residence at Chester Cathedral is a small board, with 'Beware of the Cats' on it, at the entrance to the Bishop's house. Olsen and Hansen, a Siamese chocolate point and oriental red respectively, often sit at the top of the steps, keeping a watch over the adjacent cathedral and approaching visitors.

The cathedral whose environs they survey has a chequered history: with bits in it from every century since the tenth, the cathedral has been significantly rebuilt three times. The first church, the remains of St Werbergh's, was replaced with a Norman abbey by Hugh (Lupus), Earl of Chester, as a celestial insurance policy against a somewhat wild style of life. Then, in

THE CATHEDRAL

Olsen and Hansen are not the first Danes to make their presence felt in Chester. Vikings from Denmark and Norway swept through large areas of England in the ninth and tenth centuries, and the Viking Great Army was garrisoned inside the old Roman walls of Chester during the winter of AD896, before setting off to plunder North Wales.

But in the tenth century it provided a refuge for nuns from Repton rescuing the remains of St Werburgh from an invading Danish army, and in due course the existing church was rededicated to her by Aethelflaed, daughter of Alfred the Great.

Having become a monastery it narrowly escaped destruction at Henry VIII's dissolution of the same and became a cathedral in 1541, but deteriorated thereafter – Daniel Defoe commented on the disintegration of the stonework, and only after extensive repair and restoration by Sir Gilbert Scott was the cathedral able to reopen for use in the early twentieth century.

the thirteenth century, monks built over the Norman church, to form the basis of the present-day cathedral. Olsen and Hansen live with the Bishop of Chester, the Rt Rev. Dr Peter Forster, his Danish wife Elizabeth, and their children, in a rambling Georgian building in the middle of the Cathedral Close. Olsen came to Chester with the family and his friend Murphy, a boisterous Golden Retriever. Hansen is a newcomer, and despite an initial period of deep gloom on Olsen's part at the arrival of this feline Johnny-come-lately, the two cats have reached an accord (with Murphy acting as go between). Daughter Helen's phone calls from India demonstrate the cats' importance in the family, always starting with 'Hello, how are the cats?'

After introducing himself around the cathedral close, getting locked in the free-standing 1970s bell tower, and having had his application for the position of food taster in the retreat house kitchen turned down, Olsen was tempted to dismiss the religious life. He turned instead to the lure of nights in the city, an early consequence of which was an encounter with a car; despite a broken leg, and homilies from the Bishop about the physical and moral dangers of becoming debauched, Olsen was undeterred.

Never mind that the town fathers too had in the past issued stern warnings about 'drunks, vagabonds, ladies of the night and the worst elements of society': Olsen simply found safer routes, through the cobbled alleyways, to various nocturnal assignments.

The family were naturally curious, not to say concerned, about where Olsen went, and what he got up to, during these nightly forays. His early morning behaviour was very subdued. While the house bustled with activity, with Hansen calling loudly for his breakfast to be served, Olsen would be slumped by the kitchen stove, paws over his eyes, wincing at any sharp sound. Then one day all was made clear: early one morning Olsen tottered into the house wearing a makeshift collar, into which was tucked a modest bill from the nearby Alexander's Jazz Theatre, for entrance fee, drinks and food (with three complimentary prawns). Olsen had found the ideal surroundings for his inscrutable and laid-back style: a city jazz club.

According to the club owner, Pauline Thomson, Olsen just strolled in one night and wandered round talking to customers, staff and musicians, then settled down to listen to the music. He became a regular visitor, day after day, and after a tenor sax player had decided that Olsen was a stray and might need a home, the bill was attached to Olsen as a tracing device. The family responded, but their offer of payment was refused. They were assured that Olsen was always welcome, and would continue to get complimentary entrance and alimentation! A Siamese jazz aficionado cat is a little unusual, but it isn't difficult to imagine Olsen sitting in a darkened corner – eyes half-closed – tail twitching, nursing a scotch and soda, tapping a paw to the strains of John Coltrane or Charlie Parker. Perhaps he joins in occasionally; the Siamese voice is unique.

Hansen has built up his own social life within and around the Bishop's residence, languidly and vocally joining in social occasions (although when there is food involved, he is usually accompanied by Olsen.) Hansen, being much younger, has been kept ignorant of Olsen's secret life. But as he becomes more settled, he takes increasing interest in Olsen's doings, and when he can tear himself away from the warmth of the kitchen stove, can be seen pacing around the large garden, trying to work out where Olsen goes, and how he gets there. He is relentlessly cultivating Murphy, whose loyalty to Olsen must surely crumble in the face of Hansen's wiles. So it won't be long before Olsen arrives to take his customary seat at the Jazz Theatre, only to find Hansen already there. Who knows? If the Retreat House kitchens don't need help, there is always a place at Alexander's for a hat-check cat.

Claude and Bookie
Chichester Cathedral

'Ignorant people think it's the noise which fighting cats make that is so aggravating, but it ain't so; it's the sickening grammar they use'

Mark Twain

It's not so much that Claude and Bookie fight, but there is a certain tension between them. These two cats live with Nicholas Biddle, chaplain to the Bishop of Chichester, in a quiet corner of Canon Lane.

Before studying theology, Nicholas had been a choral scholar at Hereford Cathedral, where opportunity to observe the lives of cathedral cats was confined to fleeting glimpses of their rear quarters as they scaled the garden walls of the Bishop's Palace, with Winston, the cathedral organist's dog, in hot and noisy pursuit. But coming from a home where there were seven or eight cats at any given time, Nicholas was used to seeing cats in a somewhat calmer setting. When he left for university one of these, a cat called Raindrop, was

THE CATHEDRAL

Daniel Defoe once remarked that 'I cannot say much of Chichester, in which, if six or seven good families were removed, there would not be much conversation, except what is to be found among the canons, and the dignitaries of the cathedral.' One would hope he might find the city in general much improved today, but the cathedral retains a prominent position in its cultural life.

Described by the architectural historian Nicholas Pevsner as the most English of cathedrals, Chichester Cathedral was founded in 1075. It was rebuilt at various times but retained a 14th century spire until its sudden collapse in 1861, miraculously without loss of life, and was rebuilt by the Victorian champion of restoration, Sir Gilbert Scott. Under the floor of the nave are the remains of a Roman mosaic pavement, which can be viewed through a glass window, and the cathedral also houses the grave of the composer Gustav Holst, and the Gothic 'Arundel tomb' famously referred to in Philip Larkin's poem.

Buggles, for whom Claude was a questionable addition to the attractions of Chichester Cathedral. They had some fairly vocal encounters, but Chichester Cathedral is used to loud sounds, though perhaps not so much to dissonance: music is a major feature of cathedral life. The cathedral takes pride in its eclectic musical events, from Bach to Berlioz, and from chamber music to former Rolling Stone Bill Wyman. The irrepressible Claude turned Canon Lane into his personal playground, travelling from one end to the other by hopping from parked car to parked car. Nicholas can never work out how Claude always manages to leave a trail of muddy pawprints even on a perfectly dry day, and often a double set on cars that have been recently cleaned. Canon Lane was Claude's safe haven, somewhere to relax and unwind – and then the pilgrims came. Chichester Cathedral has been a place of pilgrimage for centuries: Nicholas Pevsner's 'most English of Cathedrals' contained the shrine of St Richard of Chichester until the Reformation. But even though the remains of St Richard have been lost, a group of like-minded and very cheerful people have decided to revive the tradition of the pilgrimage.

tasked to keep Nicholas concentrated on his theological studies. When Nicholas went to take up a curacy in Bedford, Raindrop returned to the family home, and Nicholas and his wife Marieke were joined by two other cats, Claude and Minnie.

Having lost Minnie to local road traffic, a move to Chichester Cathedral, where Nicholas had been appointed Bishop's Chaplain, was doubly welcome. There would be less traffic nearby, and Claude would be free to wander, which he did with a vengeance. In the cloisters he discovered a black and white cat called

One warm summer afternoon Claude was taking a nap under a shrubbery when his sleep was abruptly ended by a hubbub of chatter and a clatter of boots, as a large group of people walked through the Canon Gate archway into the lane. Claude woke up with a start, and blearily peered out of his lair to see what all the racket was about. Just then two of the group whipped out guitars, starting to sing gustily as they made their way up the lane. Claude has a problem with music at the best of times (when Nicholas sings in the bath, he shoulders his way into the bathroom, meowing in protest) and for Claude this was too much: he stumped along the lane into the silence of his own home. Thereafter he became wary of any figure walking along the lane, for fear they might suddenly produce a guitar and start bellowing at him; he turned his attention to the gardens of the Bishop's Palace.

Claude charmed the Bishop, a frequent visitor to the Biddles' home, sitting deferentially beside him and paying courteous attention to every word the bishop spoke. This obsequious behaviour secured him special and unrestricted access to the Bishop's Palace gardens, and he now divides his time between the gardens and the cloisters, where he and Buggles compete with whoever is performing in the cathedral.
Claude was more than content to be the only household cat, and then Bookie, the last remaining cat of the Biddle feline clan (and at twenty-one this collection's oldest cat), arrived. Bookie had expected some sort of a welcome from Claude, some acknowledgement of his pre-eminence. But Claude forgot his manners, and completely ignored the new arrival. While Claude does his PR with the Bishop, Bookie sits, rather sullenly, behind the settee. There is an unspoken buffer zone between the two cats of several feet – up to thirty where space allows. There are no real confrontations, except the odd heartfelt but

ineffective swat. Bookie has become a house cat, and spends much of his time in the study, from where he can gaze wistfully at the cathedral spire. Once in a while he wanders out, and is occasionally rewarded for his efforts by the sight of Claude being pursued by an indignant Buggles, who is quite sure that the Bishop gave him sole right of access to the Palace gardens.

PREVIOUS PAGE
The irrepressible Claude
LEFT
Bookie, the old family retainer
ABOVE
Claude does excellent PR with the Bishop

Godiva and Leofric
Durham Cathedral

'Cats, as a class, have never completely got over the snootiness caused by the fact that in Ancient Egypt they were worshipped as gods'
P.G. Wodehouse

Godiva and Leofric, the cathedral cats of Durham, live in one of the most spectacular settings in Britain. The cathedral has been designated a UNESCO World Heritage Site, ranking it alongside such marvels as the pyramids and the Acropolis. Set high above the city in a loop of the River Wear, Durham Cathedral's distinctive twin towers and central tower can be seen for miles around, and in an autumnal light the whole building appears to emit a welcoming glow.

Godiva and Leofric were born to another cathedral cat – Simkin, of Salisbury Cathedral. The Dean of Durham, Michael Sadgrove, has strong connections to Salisbury, where he taught at the theological college. The death of his previous cats coincided with news

THE CATHEDRAL

Set high above the city in a loop of the River Wear, Durham Cathedral's distinctive twin west towers and the 15th century central tower are visible for many miles around, and as a UNESCO World Heritage site, rightly takes its place alongside the Acropolis, the Grand Canyon, the Pyramids and the nearby Hadrian's Wall.

This area played an important role in the early history of Christianity in Britain and Durham Cathedral houses the shrine of St Cuthbert (and fragments of his coffin) and the tomb of the Venerable Bede. The Lindisfarne Gospels once lived here too, but were removed by the King's Commissioners at the Reformation.

A large number of the original monastic buildings remain despite the depredations of the Reformation: the dormitory, refectory, (rebuilt) Chapter House, the Great Kitchen (now the cathedral bookshop) and the Deanery, formerly the prior's house.

from Salisbury that Simkin had given birth to kittens, and the Sadgroves decided that they would have two from the litter. At this time, the Sadgroves were based in Sheffield and for a while the two kittens from Salisbury had to be content with being cathedral cats-in-waiting, but not for long. With the appointment of Michael as Dean of Durham Cathedral, the family were transported from the relatively prosaic surroundings of Sheffield to the medieval splendour of the Dean's Lodgings at Durham Cathedral. The Deanery overlooks College Green at one end, has its own private door to the cathedral cloisters at the other, and is one of the oldest continuously inhabited buildings in England. It was the Prior's house in monastic times, as well as the original building of the Benedictine monastery, and with some elegant Georgian extensions could now easily be a gracious manor house in the country.

On the day after their arrival in Durham Leofric disappeared. After a fruitless search for Leofric around the house, gardens and the college green, the Sadgroves were at a loss. They couldn't think of anywhere else to look. But that evening, the household was startled by unearthly sounds floating through the house; an extensive search suggested that these ghostly noises were coming from the depths of the Deanery, and Michael, poker in hand, followed by some rather nervous children, descended into the cellars. The spectral howls grew louder as they passed into the monastic undercroft, until they were eventually tracked down to the iron grid covering the medieval latrine pit. At the sound of familiar voices the howls diminished into rather pathetic mews and Leofric, dishevelled, indignant and extremely hungry, was eventually extracted. Before long a moratorium had to be declared on jokes about Leofric trying to revive

PREVIOUS PAGE
Leofric and Godiva watch over College Green
LEFT
Leofric got lost in the medieval latrines
OPPOSITE RIGHT
Godiva on her way to a chapter house meeting

County Durham's time-honoured tradition of coal mining. A planned appearance in a *Country Life* feature eventually gave Leofric a chance to recover his dignity.

It has to be said that not everyone was overjoyed at the arrival of the cats; the chapter clerk for one, and the Dean's secretary for another. With a notable lack of the humility that characterised their Benedictine predecessors, the cats worked relentlessly to overcome this resistance, and not only does the chapter clerk now have a cat of his own, he also arranged for a gothic-style cat flap to be pierced through one of the walls at a cat-convenient height. The Dean's secretary Barbara proved more resilient, so each cat would take it in turns to sit in the in-tray on her desk, looking at her with mute reproach. 'Visits from God', she called them. No matter how many times they were shooed away, they'd return, and over time, Barbara was forced to give ground. She is still no cat lover, but tolerance is a state that cats understand: it is their attitude towards us for much of the time.

The initial encounter between Leofric and Godiva and the Archdeacon's cats exposed the fifteenth century cloisters to some fairly unecclesiastical language. In keeping with the studious and peaceful traditions of the cloisters, all the cats now avoid each other, each pair pretending that the other is invisible. Both Leofric and Godiva take their place in the twelfth century chapter house during meetings, and spend an

inordinate amount of time seeking out the most comfortable laps. This inevitably delays the start of the meetings, as it is hard to concentrate on weighty matters when one has a cat circling and prodding endlessly on one's lap, trying to find exactly the right position. And why do cats always head for the person in black?

Winston, Wallace and Cassiopeia
St Mary's Episcopal Cathedral, Edinburgh

'The smallest feline is a masterpiece'
Leonardo de Vinci

St Mary's Episcopal Cathedral sits imposingly at the centre of Palmerston Square, in Edinburgh's Georgian 'new town', the cathedral clergy and staff living nearby amidst understated Georgian elegance. Surrounded on all sides by roads, it does not seem an ideal place for cats. Yet there are some brave enough.

The Rev. Canon Jane Millard is Vice Provost of St Mary's and chaplain for the cathedral's important ministry to HIV sufferers. In the course of her work, she has helped to re-house more than thirty-three cats and thirty-two dogs. Winston was one of these: it became obvious after he had been re-housed that he was pining, so back he came. Winston wasn't too bothered by Jane's other cats, but to be in the house

THE CATHEDRAL
Set in the quiet and ordered Georgian city surroundings of Edinburgh's 'New Town', St Mary's Episcopal Cathedral is the youngest of the cathedrals featured in this book, and was the first cathedral to be built in the British Isles since the Reformation.

The cathedral's sandstone walls escaped the widespread sand-blasting of the 1980s, and so retain the same dark stonework appearance as the Walter Scott monument in Princes Street. In bad weather this presents a slightly gloomy aspect which contrasts with the many activities in which the cathedral is engaged.

In the early days the Cathedral took part in the formation of an Industrial Dwelling Company to make affordable dwellings available for labourers. One of the cathedral's more prominent domestic activities these days is its mission to AIDS sufferers.

with two friendly dogs was a new experience, as Winston's previous encounters with canines had mainly involved high-speed escapes. He was fascinated. Every where the dogs went, so did Winston. He sampled their food, drank from their water, sat in their favourite places, and ultimately took over the dog basket. The poor dogs didn't know whether they were coming or going but eventually resigned themselves to a lifetime of Winston's too-close attentions.

Winston regularly accompanied Jane to her country cottage, where he'd roam in the hills to his heart's content, fruitlessly but enthusiastically chasing deer. The travel didn't bother him, and the dogs kept him (reluctant) company. Clearly he was thoroughly unfazed by wildlife of all varieties. So when some impudent mice ran amok in the cathedral, parading among the flying buttresses and processing through the diagonal arches, Winston was appointed as Deterrent-General. However, on seeing a mouse cavorting in front of the choir, he simply sat down and began to wash himself. There was an occasion when Winston was spotted, fast asleep on a chair, with a little procession of mice tiptoeing right past. Whatever Winston got up to during his country visits, he certainly didn't bring the same attitude to St Mary's. But a pattern of visiting was established, and Winston's takes great pleasure in accompanying Jane to the cathedral, to groom himself, get warm on radiators – and steadfastly ignore the blatant posturing of the resident mice.

The foundation of the cathedral is almost entirely owing to the generosity of the two unmarried daughters of Sir Patrick Walker, Barbara and Mary Walker, who bequeathed their entire fortune to the Episcopalian Church, on the condition that a cathedral was built on their chosen site. Their interest has been taken over by Wallace & Cassiopeia, two cats who live by the cathedral in Palmerston Square. From across the road they oversee the massive central tower and choir school like sentient gargoyles. Wallace belongs to the Rev. William Mounsey, chaplain to the Royal Air Force at Leuchars, and Cassiopeia to the Rev. Dean Fosterkew, Team Vicar at the cathedral.

Wallace started out living by the airbase where William was chaplain, and loved the high octane Air Force life, delighting in being startled by the thunder of powerful jets and watching the aerobatics that were performed out over the sea. He and his fellow RAF cat, Bruce, joined gleefully in the rough and tumble of the pilots' mess: it was a life full of pranks and dares. They devised their own high jinks, the most dramatic being cattle herding. The spectacle of two cats in hot pursuit of a herd of nervous bullocks became a regular feature of local farming life. The RAF Leuchars posting meant a more domestic location, and Bruce promptly moved out. Upon the move to the more tranquil surroundings of St Mary's Cathedral Wallace was warmly welcomed by Cassiopeia, which was some kind of compensation.

Cassiopeia, a half Burmese, is a bit of a great-aunt cat – a cat that could wear lorgnettes, who spends much time tutting good-naturedly at the high spirits shown by the cathedral choristers as they passed on the way to the cathedral. Cassiopeia had turned the sitting room balcony into her personal review platform and local office workers called out greetings as they made their way to work, as did the choristers, postman, and casual passers-by. Cassiopeia responds to all and sundry with a regal nod. After she had explained the proper rules of conduct, Wallace eagerly joined her for the daily review of those passing, and responds to the choristers' cheerful greetings with an equally cheerful meow. When Wallace gets too familiar with people in the street, Cassiopeia fusses him inside and reminds him of the cathedral cats' code of decorum.

Hamish, Dilly, Suajeta, Scheherazade, Harry and Boots
Ely Cathedral

'The really great thing about cats is their endless variety. One can pick a cat to fit almost any kind of decor, color, scheme, income, personality, mood'

Eric Gurney

Under the gaze of the unique octagonal tower of Ely Cathedral, its cathedral cats spend a lot of time in negotiation: all argue that they have (more or less) legitimate claims to their territories, and concessions are reached only after extensive and noisy discussion. Veteran cathedral cats Marmaduke and Skimbleshanks used to have the cathedral pretty much to themselves. But now Ely Cathedral is home to a chorus of cats, all with their own particular territories.

The only things that can unite the Ely Cathedral cats are incursions by outside cats or a badly behaved dog. Then they form a cohort of which Oliver Cromwell, who lived in Ely, would have been proud. So, who are these Johnny-come-lately's at Ely? Well, there's

THE CATHEDRAL

Known as the 'the ship of the Fens', Ely Cathedral dominates the flat fenland landscape. It was built on the site of a Saxon convent founded by Ethelreda; the present church was begun in the 11th century, with cathedral status being granted in 1109.

After the collapse of the original Norman central tower, Alan of Walsingham had a moment of creative inspiration, and designed an octagonal tower, rather than a conventional four-sided one.

Cromwell used the cathedral to stable his cavalry, which may be why Ely Cathedral survived the Civil War relatively unscathed; but the dissolution of the monasteries and the Reformation took their toll, including the loss of St Ethelreda's much-visited shrine.

Ely retains a large number of former monastic medieval buildings still in domestic use: the Great Gateway; Prior Crauden's chapel; the Chapter House; the Black Hostelry; and Powcher's Hall. These buildings are used today by the Kings School and the cathedral community.

PREVIOUS PAGE
Clockwise from top left: Suajeta, Dilly,
Harry and Scheherazade
LEFT
Hamish, one of the cacophony of
Ely cats
OPPOSITE RIGHT
Boots, an expert ladder climber

Hamish, a polydactyl (six-toed) ginger fellow who lives with the verger, Martin Fleet, his wife Paula, and their two children, Charlotte and Lawrence. Their house is part of a long Victorian terrace incorporating the original thirteenth century undercroft; next to them lives the cathedral Bursar Stephen Wikner and his wife Stefanie, with their two cats Boots and Harry; next to them live Marmaduke and Skimbleshanks, the veteran cats of the cathedral organist and his family. It is this domestic proximity that has originated intense on-going feline discussions about land rights. The territory under dispute takes in the largest collection of medieval buildings still in domestic use: the Chapter House, Powcher's Hall and the Black Hostelry (so named after the black habits worn by the Benedictine monks). The Ely Cathedral cats range

without hindrance from the Great Gateway (at one time a gaol, and more recently an ale-house), through the King's School grounds, the Dean's Meadow and Ely Park and, further away, down to the banks of the River Great Ouse.

The first trouble came when Hamish, being naturally curious about his neighbours, poked his head through a gap in Marmaduke's and Skimbleshank's garden, to find himself face to face with both cats. All that could be seen on Hamish's side was his rear quarters, tail fluffed up in alarm, frantically trying to back out. On the other side Hamish's head, ears flat, stuck out of the gap in the fence faced an equally alarmed Skimbleshanks and Marmaduke. Hamish fled back to his house with the two other cats in hot pursuit. There followed some pretty inappropriate exchanges; insults and recriminations rebounded, and then Harry and Boots made their entrance.

Stephen Wikner is an old hand with cats. He had travelled widely with his various cats, and one of them even accompanied him on an epic sea journey from South Africa to Scotland. When Harry and Boots came rushing back to their home, he devised a safe entry and exit route for them.

One might be forgiven for wondering whether a cat flap in the window of a first-floor bathroom is generally a Good Thing, but it was only one element in a more elaborate plan. The cat flap would only respond to a magnetic collar, and opened onto a ladder; the ladder led to a tree, and only thence to the ground. Harry and Boots were duly fitted out with their magnetic collars, and were able to sally forth at

some height, while if the need arose for hasty retreat, both cats could scramble up and the flap would slam shut in the face of their pursuers.

Dilly, Scheherazade and Suajeta live with their family, the Porter-Thaws, around the other side of the cathedral, in what is now the Choir House: they avoid the more rumbustious areas inhabited by Harry et al., preferring the cover afforded by the old monastic buildings and cathedral offices. These are the laid-back cats of Ely, who prefer to flop around listening to music, hanging out with choristers and music students. Marmaduke and Skimbleshanks don't come calling – they have more than enough music in their own house. Hamish, Harry and Boots, on the other hand, have all tried to get in, and have been summarily ejected from the Porter-Thaws' garden. They glare through the hedge at Dilly, Scheherazade and Suajeta, and at one another, then wander off to pick an argument with Skimbleshanks and Marmaduke. There have been accidental encounters, as when all the cats converged unintentionally at the Galilee Porch (a fine example of Early English architecture). This noisy affair was dealt with in a firm but fair manner by the vigilant vergers, who had already dealt with one cat emergency – Harry had been accidentally locked in, and spent an unhappy night curled up near the stone slab marking the place where St Etheldreda's shrine stood. He has now forsworn the cathedral and has taken to mooching around by the river; it remains to be seen what he makes of the swans.

Emma and Thomas
Exeter Cathedral

'I believe cats to be spirits come to earth. A cat, I am sure, could walk on a cloud without coming through'

Jules Verne

Whether the nursery rhyme 'Hickory Dickory Dock' really did have its origins at Exeter Cathedral is disputable, but the 15th century astronomical clock in the North Transept does have some interesting features: built by a Glastonbury monk, the workings of this clock would have been greased with animal fat – particularly appetizing to mice. In the doorway that gives access to the clock there is a crude hole, reputedly made to give access to a cat in hot pursuit of these horological rodents! And medieval archives show that there was a cat on the cathedral staff, who received a weekly payment of one penny.

Thomas came into Canon Neil Collins's life as a result of a wedding he presided at during his time as a vicar

THE CATHEDRAL

Exeter Cathedral was built in the Romanesque style by William the Conqueror's nephew William Warelwast, but underwent substantial reconstruction in the 13th century, inspired by the newly-built gothic cathedral at Salisbury – only the towers were retained from the Norman version.

The cathedral has had a turbulent history, beginning with the damage inflicted by the besieging forces of King Stephen in 1136, via the demolishment of the cloisters under Cromwell, to a direct hit from a German bomb during one of the so-called 'Baedeker raids'. Under the Parliamentarian governor Colonel Hammond, the cathedral had to be partitioned by a brick wall in order to allow Presbyterian and Congregationalist congregations to worship at the same time.

Despite its troubles Exeter Cathedral retains some notable features, with the longest unbroken ceiling vaulting in the country in the nave and choir and a rich variety of sculpture and carving.

by his shoulder, murmuring persuasive words in his ear. On arriving home Canon Collins consulted Joan, his cat sitter, as to whether Emma would mind another cat. She thought a ginger cat might be a fine companion; Emma was very maternal and, reasoned Joan, would welcome the opportunity to use her motherly traits. And so it proved, with the cats developing a relationship rather like that of AA Milne's Kanga and Tigger – maternal and calm versus irrepressible and bouncy. Emma found it a little tiring, and sometimes found Thomas quite exasperating, but the two cats had formed an enduring friendship by the time they came to Exeter Cathedral, where Neil became Canon Treasurer.

in Harpenden. The bride and groom were vets, and during the reception engaged Neil Collins in a lengthy conversation about their need to re-house an amiable stray ginger tomcat. Canon Collins, slightly taken aback, gently admonished the newlyweds that perhaps they ought to have more immediate matters to attend to, and thought no more about it during the rest of the wedding reception. But on the long drive home through a winter dusk he recalled the conversation about the cat and it was almost as if the cat was sitting

It was Advent Sunday when they all arrived at the late fourteenth century Canon's house overlooking the Cathedral green. Thomas and Emma spent the first few days creeping around anxiously, but in due course they relaxed. Thomas spent hours gazing curiously from the first floor sitting room window at the swirl of life outside – passers-by, the postman, and a continuous stream of visitors entering and leaving the cathedral. But Emma didn't care for the bustle of outside life, and if Neil conversed for too long by the front door, Emma's head would emerge through the cat flap, and she'd miaow reproachfully.

For Thomas, though, just looking was not enough, and he soon made his first forays further afield. The cobbled lane in front of the house is traffic-free, and there he could roll and stretch to his heart's content, and what more dramatic backdrop than the decorated gothic nave of Exeter Cathedral, with its imposing twin Norman towers (minus its original 'pepperpot' spires, lost to King Stephen's gunners in the twelfth century.) The green was frequented by visitors who often had food: Thomas became proficient at sniffing out that most pungent of English dishes, fish and chips. He became adept at slipping into the cathedral, where he discovered the safe haven of the medieval clock, and the terrors of a jubilant organ voluntary. Thomas acquired a circle of admirers who would make a point of coming to see him, and was transformed into a rumbustious dandy. He was swept away by all the adulation: why, the whole of the city was at his feet. Thomas set out to bring the message of his glorious felinity wide and far. Not all paths lead home, and one particular promenade took him past Mol's Coffee Shop – once frequented by Sir Francis Drake and Sir Walter Raleigh – out into the swirl of the High Street – and there he got lost. A frantic search discovered a slightly chastened Thomas a few days later, at the Exeter Cats Protection League. His tales of glory had been met with scepticism by the other cats in protective custody. For a while he was chastened,

but with the news of his adventure a local newspaper published his photograph, and there was a postcard of him on sale in the cathedral bookshop: he was soon back to his old ways. Inside the house, though, Thomas plays to the gallery in a different way, feigning such helplessness that Emma, brushing aside her irritation at his public antics, still mothers and fusses around him, as though he were still the bouncy but vulnerable cat that first came to the vicarage at Harpenden.

Bonnie & Flora
Gloucester Cathedral

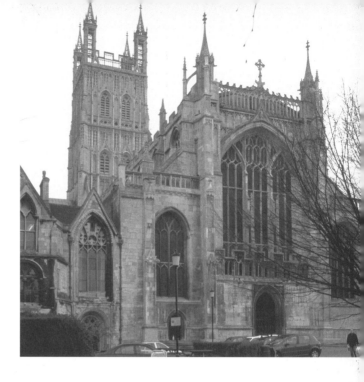

'A cat's got her own opinion of human beings. She don't say much, but you can tell enough to make you anxious not to hear the whole of it'

Jerome K. Jerome

There is a great tradition of cats in Gloucester. Dick Wittington's cat is supposed to have come from here, and legend has it that all the cats of the city speak to each other on Christmas Eve. The cathedral has also a lively tradition of resident cats: Gorbachov, featured in the first Cathedral Cats book, who was succeeded by Maud, who in turn handed over the post to Bonnie. Gloucester Cathedral stands out as a beacon of history and heritage in a city that, in the 1960s, did its best to cover everything in a deluge of concrete: the contrast between the cathedral, its 11 acres of precincts, and the surrounding 'high street'-style shopping areas is extraordinary. For a resident cat, the close offers opportunities for passing friendships, peaceful strolls and, more importantly, snacks.

THE CATHEDRAL

Gloucester Cathedral is a beacon of history and heritage in a city that, courtesy of the 1960s, is otherwise a nightmare of concrete. Construction of the present building began in the late 11th century, and despite disastrous fires, the collapse of the Southern tower and the uncertainties of the civil war between Empress Matilda and King Stephen, the building was in generally good repair by the time of the coronation at the cathedral of Henry III, in 1216.

The cloisters here are the next best thing to a working monastery, with the stone alcoves where the monks studied, as well as the lavatorium, complete with stone towel alcove. In the cathedral itself, the Great East window is a spectacular example of medieval stained glass, almost the size of a tennis court.

Edward II's burial at Gloucester after his murder helped it escape the excesses of Henry VIII's dissolution of the monasteries, given his respect for his ancestor's tomb. Pilgrims visiting the tomb partly financed the perpendicular-style choir and presbytery.

Canon residentiary David Hoyle came to Gloucester about two years ago, with his wife Janet, daughter Katy and Bonnie the cat. Bonnie had led a settled life in London, and didn't take at all kindly to being relocated. Within a very short while of arriving, Bonnie moved out. Despite a thorough and persistent search, there was no sign of her – she simply vanished, and after a month Katy had given up hope of ever seeing Bonnie again.

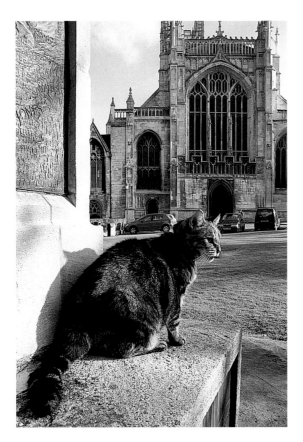

In the meantime, Janet Hoyle's sister Helen had come to live with them in the cathedral close, bringing with her a wide-eyed and jumpy black and white cat by the name of Flora. Flora took to life at the cathedral with even less enthusiasm than Bonnie; at the first opportunity she fled into a maze of medieval cellars and drains beneath the house. Trying to rescue a cat that wants to be rescued is hard enough, but trying to rescue a cat that doesn't want to be rescued is nearly impossible. In the end, after a lot of cajoling, pleading, and possibly just a little prodding, Flora re-emerged into daylight.

Daughter Katy had made new friends in Gloucester, and one afternoon made her way to a friend's home, where she was welcomed and shown into the sitting room. On the window sill, looking a bit shamefaced but in very good shape, was Bonnie. What a fickle cat. After a slightly tense reunion, and many explanations, Bonnie was returned to her rightful owner, only to find that her place had apparently been taken by another cat who was nothing more than a bag of nerves. Bonnie wasn't having this, and at the first opportunity she wandered off again, and moved in with another local family. It was the verger's ginger cat Tinker who sorted things out. He pointed out to her some of the many advantages of life as a cathedral cat, not the least of which were the tidbits that could be cadged from unwary visitors. Bonnie relented, returning home for a reconciliation with her family.

Tinker's advice was sound; Bonnie found that people regularly come to eat a snack lunch in the calm of the cathedral close, and though clearly far from being malnourished, she developed a piteous miaow alongside her rampant appetite for chips. And the cathedral precincts offered the chance for adulation too: tucked away in a shady alley is a tiny shop, made famous by Beatrix Potter in 'The Tailor of Gloucester'. This little shop, now preserved by the National Trust, is a honey pot for Beatrix Potter fans from all over the world, and Bonnie is the star of the show, masquerading as Simkin outside the tailor's shop. Local people have seen Bonnie lolling around the cathedral, but overseas visitors are completely taken in: cameras click, videos roll, and people are enchanted by what they believe to be the living embodiment of the Tailor of Gloucester's Simkin.

Bonnie and Tinker regularly pass the time of day in the cathedral cloisters, where, in monastic times, the young novices would play games such as Nine Men's Morris (the markings can been seen scratched into the stone work). The cloisters are renowned for the fan vaulting too, a style of stonework pioneered at Gloucester. The two cats were not at all pleased to be kept out by the Harry Potter film crew; they were not sinister enough to justify a walk-on performance, besides which they kept making the extras giggle. Inside the cathedral the bookshop offers sympathy, attention, and more importantly a comfortable radiator shelf. And Bonnie regularly sits on David

Hoyle's knees during evensong, cocking a critical ear at the choir, and joins official processions (graciously permitting the Bishop to walk in front of her). The only thing likely to send her running for home is the sonorous booming of Great Peter, Britain's only remaining medieval bell, as it rings out over the city.

PREVIOUS PAGE
Bonnie strikes a pose
OPPOSITE LEFT
Bonnie is now a consummate
performer
ABOVE
Flora had no interest in being rescued
from the cellars

Saffron and Mevagissey
Hereford Cathedral

'It always gives me a shiver when I see a cat seeing what I can't see'

Eleanor Farjeon

Saffron and Mevagissey arrived in this world in unusual circumstances. Their parents, Cable and Wireless, had been taken for neutering at four months; the only problem was that one of them, Wireless, was already pregnant. The two kittens were given to Peter Dyke, the assistant cathedral organist, and installed in the cloister house shared with Shaun Ward, director of the Diocesan Organist Training Scheme.

There are two cloisters at Hereford Cathedral: the fifteenth century Bishop's Cloister, which is open to the public, and the College Cloisters, so called because they originally housed the Vicars Choral, who sang in the cathedral choir. It was here that Mevagissey and Saffron came, a mischievous pair of kittens.

THE CATHEDRAL

The rose-coloured sandstone of Hereford Cathedral is in harmony with the red soil of this traditionally farming-centred county. Like so many cathedrals, it has been rebuilt to various extents at different times, and has known both good times and bad in tandem with the rise and fall of the diocese's power and influence.

For example, only fragments remain of the once gloriously-vaulted, ten-sided Chapter House, but a sketch made in the early 18th century shows the splendour of its Decorated style. The cathedral began to decay after the rigours of the Civil War and Reformation, with the eventual collapse of the entire west end, restored only in the last century.

Never a monastic establishment, for the best part of twelve centuries the cathedral here has comprised three main elements: the church; its library; and its school. Today, two of Britain's most important historical treasures, the Mappa Mundi and Chained Library, are proudly displayed in the new library at Hereford.

The two cats have inherited a large area of the cathedral precincts from their predecessor Princess, to which they have added the Bishop's Palace Gardens, the deanery, and a vast swathe of lawn running down to the River Wye. Here they sometimes sit, on branches overhanging the river, gazing longingly at the procession of ducks and coots swimming up and down.

The West Front of the cathedral, however, is unknown to the cats: the close has proved to be the most hazardous area of the cathedral for Saffron and Mevagissey, as they have had to run the gauntlet of the gimlet-eyed dog belonging to the cathedral organist, Dr Roy Massey. This is a time-honoured tradition of feline life at Hereford Cathedral. The cats do not like the rush and bustle of Broad Street so visits to the new cathedral library building, which houses the world-famous Mappa Mundi and chained library, are off the agenda. Even if Mevagissey and Saffron were to find their way to the library, its strict no-animal policy would ensure their exclusion. They can wander into the cathedral from the Bishops Cloister, but it requires a very precise sense of timing, as the door is pulled closed by a very heavy spring.

One of the first excursions made by Saffron and Mevagissey was to the Choir School, also housed in the College Cloisters: they clambered up an old pear tree onto the cloister roof, on which they scrambled and slipped their way around, until they heard singing. The two kittens (as they were then) lowered themselves backwards down the tiles until they reached a gutter, from which they managed to get onto a high window ledge, from where, finally, they could see what was happening inside. The choristers were busy at their various tasks, and no one noticed two white kittens cautiously wriggling through a cracked pane of glass and along the window ledge. Saffron and Mevagissey spent quite a time watching and listening before deciding that they wanted to join in: the only problem was that there was no easy way down. So began the first of a series of wild leaps that is still characteristic of the way that they dash about the cathedral: both Saffron and Mevagissey launched themselves into the air, one landing in a heap on a pile of music, the other catching the edge of a music stand – which promptly collapsed to the floor, with the kitten hanging on for dear life. Choir practice dissolved into chaos: no one sure at first if they had been the victims of an assault by cathedral imps, or what! Order was eventually restored, and the kittens, chastened by the after-effects of their swashbuckling entrance, were soothed and fussed over while a chorister was dispatched with a polite note to Peter asking if he would please collect his new kittens.

The scaffolding on the Lady Chapel has provided Saffron with endless hours of fun, as has a large yew tree: visitors and staff are often startled by the ghostly vision of two white cats stretched out along its branches, inscrutably surveying their domain. These cats do get around; they seem to have a window

fixation. At a year old Saffron wandered off, and was found living on the third floor of the Deanery, under a bed, and even now often clambers into the adjacent verger's house through an upstairs bedroom window. Domestic life has its dramas too. The cats' house in the cloisters has an extra and uninvited occupant – the ghost of one John Constable, butler to the college, who died in mysterious circumstances. Saffron and Mevagissey have been frequently startled by locked windows suddenly rushing open, and by the unexplained banging of doors.

Ghosts apart, home life is entertaining: as a kitten Mevagissey liked to sleep inside the grand piano, on the strings. Only a vigorous exercise in chromatic scales would dislodge her, and she still sits gazing in fascination at the rise and fall of the hammers, putting out a tentative exploratory paw every now and then. Saffron prefers the collection of period string instruments scattered about the house, and occasionally takes a tentative pluck at their strings (thankfully unaware that they are made from cat gut!).

Saffron and Mevagissey have no established routine for casual visits; the only place that receives their regular attention is the office of the Cathedral Perpetual Trust, where food is set out in anticipation; but even then they won't enter through the door, only a window. The only rooms that Saffron and Mevagissey enter via the door are those in their own house, and committee meeting rooms, where they will follow Peter or Shaun, looking around for a lap to sit on, preferably belonging to someone wearing sombre black, so as to show off to best effect the white hairs they leave!

There is one particular cupboard, constructed to cover the remains of a fifteenth century doorway, that Mevagissey sits and stares at for hours on end: sometimes she appears relaxed, and at other times her hackles rise inexplicably. This was part of a first floor gallery along which the butler would regularly walk. These two white cats have something of a ghostly appearance themselves, of course, especially when seen from across the cloisters, sitting motionless in the frame of a gothic weathered sandstone archway.

Kim and Boris
Lichfield Cathedral

'To respect the cat is the beginning of the aesthetic sense'

Erasmus Darwin

A close examination of the cathedral staff photo at Lichfield Cathedral reveals, peering out from between the feet of cathedral groundsman Mark Jervis, a wiry and determined-looking grey cat. This is Kim, unofficial sovereign of Lichfield Cathedral, and official cathedral cat. She lives with Mark in a cottage which, as it happens, is opposite what was Erasmus Darwin's herb garden, within the cathedral close.

Inside the cathedral there is a handsome memorial to Darwin, whose herb garden provides such rich scents for Kim, where the city's intellectual traditions are also handsomely acknowledged by memorials to Samuel Johnson and David Garrick. As befits a cathedral that stands in a city celebrated by Daniel Defoe for its 'good

THE CATHEDRAL

Lichfield Cathedral's three distinctive spires are instantly recognizable, as are the ranks of carved figures that ornament the cathedral's west front, and the city's intellectual traditions are handsomely acknowledged by memorials to Samuel Johnson, David Garrick and Erasmus Darwin.

The first church here was a Saxon cathedral, built by Bishop Hedda in 700, to house the remains of St Chad. Though built over long since, recent archeology has produced more knowledge about the extent of the Saxon cathedral, and has also revealed what may have been St Chad's original burial chamber.

Lichfield Cathedral lost its status as a see after the Norman invasion (Coventry took over), but an early Norman bishop, Roger de Clinton, rebuilt the cathedral, fortified the close and provided renewed facilities for pilgrims. The octagonal Chapter House houses an exhibition of one of the cathedral's great treasures, the 8th century Lichfield Gospels.

PREVIOUS PAGE
Kim waits for the bishop
LEFT
Kim, always under-awed by her surroundings
OPPOSITE RIGHT
Boris comes off the night shift

conversation and good company', Lichfield Cathedral takes its place in a thoroughly contemporary manner at the heart of the annual Lichfield Music Festival, during which its imposing nave echoes with an eclectic and inspiring series of concerts, recitals and performances. But this means little to Kim, who is a true one-person cat, with strict limits on the time she has available for visitors. Kim is a pure-bred farm cat, born among the rough and tumble of sheepdogs and livestock, and there is little that she needs to be taught about survival: Kim rules the cathedral close with claws of iron, acting as if Lichfield Cathedral was an extensive farm, with one particularly large and ornate barn.

Boris, her so-called companion, is a simpler soul. He came as company for Kim, despite her having made it quite clear to Mark that she neither wanted, needed nor would stand for the idea of another cat in the house. Despite Kim's objections, Boris came. A rather pleasant chap really, who tried at first to win Kim over, by bringing her various indescribable offerings. After countless protracted and vigorous disputes about food, bedding, which entrance to use, where each cat was allowed to go, what radiator belonged to who, which cat got to lie in front of the fire, who got to sit on Mark's lap and so forth, an exhausted and exasperated Mark calmed the situation by devising a shift system. Boris was sent out for the night shift, patrolling the cathedral close, and doing all the unmentionable things that cats do at night; he comes back to the house after breakfast. Kim got the day shift – which fitted with the routine she had already established: she leaves the house through the front door at the exact moment Boris comes in through the front window. The only continuing source of disagreement between the two cats now is whether it is permitted for Boris to sleep on Kim's cushion and vice versa. Perversely each cat insists on sleeping on the other's bedding.

Setting aside the complications of domestic life, Kim has another curious trait: she is the feline equivalent of a working dog, displaying a dog-like loyalty to Mark, trotting at his heels round the grounds and through the cathedral: she comes to a whistle (which she can hear over a quarter of a mile), and she keeps livestock in check – by which one is understood to refer to visiting dogs. What Kim lacks in size is more than

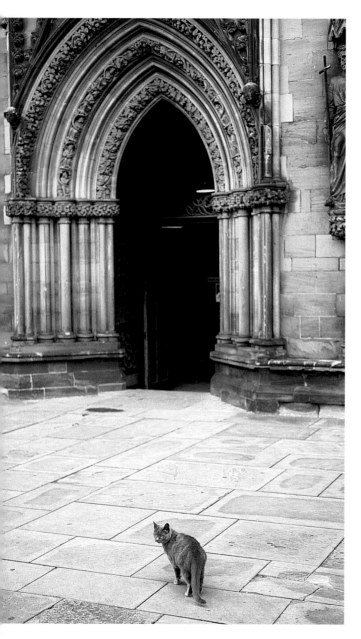

made up for in determination and the ability to surprise. Even large dogs flinch when they hear a rustling in the lavender bushes beside the path, and small dogs leap quivering into their owners' arms. Not that Kim is unnecessarily violent – she just likes to run a tight ship, and dogs, well… dogs are untidy. I imagine that no animals are involved at the childrens' Christmas crib ceremonies – any donkey with an ounce of sense would know that it would be courting disaster to disturb Kim from an afternoon rest in the crib.

In Kim's mind there was never a question of whether or not she would be permitted to go into the cathedral. As a kitten her favourite spot was the Bishop's Throne; she still curls up there, but is otherwise quite content hopping from chair to chair in the west end of the Gothic nave. Her technique is simple – walk straight in, down the gothic nave, look straight ahead, and appear to be doing something official. No one questioned it, and Kim became a regular feature of the cathedral.

Nowadays Kim's favourite spot in the cathedral is the heating grate in front of Skidmore's ornate Victoria choir screen. She doesn't mind what's going on, as long as it doesn't disturb her. She even has a seat at the back of the nave from which she can peer down towards the altar during services. Kim has a great sense of occasion, but whether she wants to feature or simply demystify proceedings is debatable. At the recent ceremony of enthronement for the new Bishop, Jonathan Gledhill, Kim was passing the west door; noticing the Head Verger knocking at the great West Door with the Bishop beside him, Kim walked up to see what they were doing. Inside, the congregation was waiting expectantly: the great West Doors swung open, and in stalked Kim, tail held high, closely followed by the Bishop and his entourage. She led the procession to the Eagle Lectern, and took her seat for the rest of the ceremony. It was the first thing that the Bishop referred to in his sermon, and earned Kim a mention in the regional press.

There are a few choice friends that Kim visits: she often calls into to see Pauline Hawkins in the cathedral offices (which just happen to be next to the cathedral coffee shop). But more often than not, Kim can be seen sitting behind Mark, on a small tractor, like one of those sheep dogs in a farm trailer that one follows endlessly down twisting country lanes.

LEFT
Kim on dog patrol
RIGHT
**From time to time Kim checks that
Boris is not sleeping in her bed**

Ivor
Portsmouth Cathedral

'It is difficult to obtain the friendship of a cat. It is a philosophical animal… one that does not place its affections thoughtlessly'
Théophile Gautier

Ivor, a genial white and ginger cat with an unusual retroussé nose, lives in a pleasantly ramshackle Georgian house next to Portsmouth cathedral with the cathedral organist David Price and his wife Kitty. Although Ivor was born on a farm, he turned out more of a meals-on-wheels cat than a farm-bred kitten.

When he came to Portsmouth the two senior family cats, Finzi and Walton (named after the English composers) were not too pleased to have a slacker around the house; after a while Ivor learned that if he wanted something, he'd have to get it himself, otherwise Finzi and Walton would either eat it, play with it or sleep on it. And they were bigger than Ivor. Ivor's home overlooks the east end of the cathedral,

THE CATHEDRAL

Portsmouth Cathedral has been a place of worship for sea-farers since it was first built, and until 1828 naval officers taking up their first command were required to take communion here.

The cathedral is based around the original chapel of St Thomas of Canterbury which was built in 1170 by a Norman land-owner, Jean de Gisor, features of which are still visible in the present cathedral.

The town's inhabitants were excommunicated and the church closed in the 15th century when local sailors murdered the Bishop of Chichester. The Civil War also took its toll – its tower doubled as a lighthouse and lookout and was an obvious target for Parliamentary gunners.

In 1927 the Diocese of Portsmouth was created and what had begun as a humble chapel for Augustinian monks became a cathedral.

and from the first floor there is a fine view of the eleventh century chancel and transept, surmounted by a tower with a distinctive wooden cupola. (The cupola is something of a curiosity: in years gone by it served as a navigation aid for shipping – complete with lantern.) For a year Ivor couldn't be bothered to go out, but one day he spotted Daisy, a neighbouring lady cat of apparently easy virtue. After only the briefest of encounters, Daisy dumped Ivor, but the episode had served to get Ivor out of the house, and he now started to take a more active interest in cathedral goings-on. Initial visits were confined to the cathedral offices, housed in a cloister-like corridor on the north side of the cathedral, where Ivor was regularly entertained by the cathedral administrator Tom Morton, Commodore RN (rtd) and his tales of life on the high seas. From here it was a short stroll to the vergers' office, where Ivor initiated a regular series of lengthy discussions with the vergers, usually on the topic of what was in the vergers' well-stocked refrigerator, and would they mind if he took a peek?

Eventually Ivor found his way into the cathedral, where one of his first acts was to test out the acoustics, now a regular activity for him; to their credit, the good folk who worship here don't bat an eyelid when their prayers and contemplations are punctuated by a series of plaintive miaows, usually in the key of A minor. Ivor also found a great position from which to observe the daily rounds of cathedral life – the comfort of the William and Mary Bishop's Chair. Around this time

PREVIOUS PAGE
Ivor tries out a new voluntary
ABOVE
The Bishop's chair makes a good vantage point
OPPOSITE LEFT
A chat with the vergers is always welcome
OPPOSITE RIGHT
A rummage around the font is the nearest that Ivor can get to a dry dock

Ivor also started to go out of the house to greet the cathedral choristers, whom he now regularly accompanies to evensong. Wailing happily along with the boy choristers, Ivor joins in a variety of musical services with gusto. Evensong remains one of his favourites and he likes to sit in the canons' stalls. But he is not partial to fortissimo: the occasional resounding Gloria sends Ivor leaping for cover, but when the noise dies down, he re-emerges from the shadows for a vigorous wash on the Bishop's throne. From choral singing it was a short leap to joining in childrens' workshops and other cathedral activities, which he clearly regards as an important part of his official responsibilities.

Ivor had often looked up at the organ loft, housed in the north tower, and one day David found Ivor sitting at his side gazing with intense curiosity at the manuals and stops. These days Ivor often waits for an oppor-tunity to dash up the stairs, and is to be found putting a tentative paw onto the great organ manual. It is even rumoured that he is trying to work out the difference between the Diapason Magna and the Flute Dolce.

There are however, some words of caution for Ivor regarding his desirable post as official cathedral cat. David and Kitty Price kindly introduced the head verger, Ian Griffiths, to the cat rescue agency they have used in the past, and Ian brought home with him two young cats – Scampi and Chips. At the moment they are a little timid, but guess what, Ivor? They spend most of their days sitting at a first floor window, looking at the cathedral entrance. Now, does that sound familiar?

Samson and Delilah
Ripon Cathedral

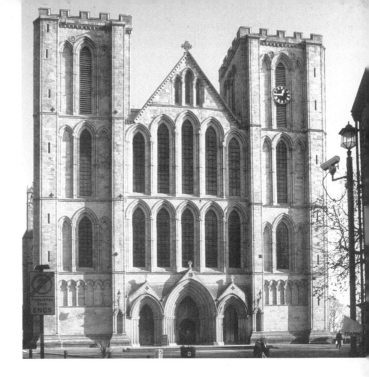

'It is a very inconvenient habit of kittens that, whatever you say to them, they always purr'

Lewis Carroll

Samson and Delilah, the family cats of John Methuen, the Dean of Ripon, and his wife Bridgit, pointedly ignore the Dean's claim to be more of a dog person than cat person. Delilah, the bolder of the two cats, leads regular incursions into the Dean's study, particularly when there are visitors or meetings, and plants herself emphatically in the centre of the room, from which position she looks around as if to say 'What are you going to do about it?' In the event, the Dean does nothing, and can frequently be seen with a cat on his lap, looking pretty relaxed – for a man who prefers dogs.

Lewis Carroll was a frequent visitor to Ripon Cathedral (his father was a residentiary canon there)

THE CATHEDRAL

Possibly the most striking aspect of Ripon Cathedral is the newly-restored Early English West Front – the warmth of the sandstone used in its construction gives it a welcoming glow. The original church of St Peter, a Roman-style basilica, was built in the seventh century by St Wilfrid, and the crypt is still preserved under the medieval minster. The present church building is the fourth to occupy the site, and became the cathedral church of the diocese of Ripon in 1836.

An extensive collection of misericords and carved bench ends includes the famous 'rabbit hole' misericord, which is claimed to have played a part in inspiring Lewis Carroll, son of a residentiary canon of the cathedral, to write *Alice's Adventures in Wonderland*.

The great English war poet Wilfrid Owen, posted to Ripon suffering from shellshock, wrote two of his great masterpieces here, 'Futility', and the profoundly moving 'Strange Meeting'.

and the intriguing range of carved bench ends and misericords may have helped Carroll to invent one of literature's most celebrated felines, the Cheshire Cat. The Victorian architect Sir George Gilbert Scott certainly thought so, for, during his major restoration works, he depicted the Cheshire Cat in the South Transept.

Samson and Delilah originally arrived with the Methuens' daughter, who was in transit for London, and the family decided that life would be safer for the kittens at Ripon. The same daughter's London home includes a resident German Shepherd and a Doberman which come to visit at Ripon, and although Samson and Delilah are politely hospitable, they are not too upset when it is time for the dogs to bounce back to London. The most unwelcome visitor to the house was another cat, a piratical tomcat who would poke his head through the cat flap, shouldering his way into the kitchen as if he lived there and gobbling up any available cat or dog food before settling down to a vigorous wash in the middle of the kitchen floor. As the two kittens grew, Delilah led forays from the kittens' hiding place beside the washing machine, fighting off the tom eventually, with Samson watching timidly. Most unlike their biblical namesakes!

PREVIOUS PAGE
Samson – not the most courageous of cats
LEFT
Delilah worries that the mechanical hand might still get her
OPPOSITE RIGHT
One visit to the cathedral was one too many for Delilah

Both cats developed an unerring sense of the inappropriate, seeking out visitors who were not so keen on cats, and those who came in black: these unfortunates would be gifted with special and unceasing attention, and the only real rivalry between Samson and Delilah has been over who can clamber onto a reluctant lap first.

With nothing much to worry them inside the house, the cats sought adventure further afield. The wall separating the Deanery garden and cathedral churchyard was easily climbed from the garden, but there was rather more of a drop on the cathedral side, and even after some time Samson would only go as far as the top of the wall. Delilah, on the other hand, was eager to explore the 'far side'. Her wanderings were normally restricted to the churchyard, but one cold winter's afternoon, Delilah's curiosity led her to the West door of the cathedral, and as a late visitor came out, she slipped in.

Avoiding the attention of the vergers, Delilah made her way up the nave, passing through the fifteenth century pulpitum into the chancel, where a choir practice was in progress, prior to evensong. Shortly after, the organist noticed that the choristers were not concentrating: the younger members kept breaking into fits of giggles. Peering down from the organ loft the organist spotted Delilah, alternately winding her way through the choristers' legs, and hopping along the choir stalls. In desperation, the organist reached

for a lever that operating a seventeenth century mechanical hand, used in days gone by to conduct the choir from the organ loft. This caught Delilah's attention: she gazed up nervously at this disembodied hand, creaking up and down with increasing vigour, and after one particularly wild and clattering gesture, her nerve broke, and Delilah beat a hasty retreat, startling the verger with her plaintive pleas for the door to be opened. Once outside, she tore past a startled Samson, still waiting anxiously in the tree, and tumbled back over the wall into the safety of the deanery. And that was that. Both cats prowl the Deanery gardens, and Delilah mooches around the churchyard, but there is no way she is ever going to face the phantom hand of Ripon Cathedral again.

Figaro
Rochester Cathedral

'What greater gift than the love of a cat?'
Charles Dickens

Rochester Cathedral, the second oldest cathedral foundation in Britain, stands between the old Roman Watling Street (now Rochester High Street), the imposing Norman castle, and the old Roman Wall. The strategic position of the town on the River Medway, near the coast, made it a scene of conflict from the times of the Viking invasions through to the Civil War and the cathedral suffered heavy damage from fire on several occasions – scorch marks from 12th century fires can still be seen on some pillars.

The Norman archbishop Gundulf was charged with the rebuilding of Rochester Cathedral, and this may account for the survival of much of the original Romanesque architecture, for Gundulf founded the

THE CATHEDRAL

The second oldest cathedral foundation in England, Rochester Cathedral has survived successive conflicts and fire. It was built by the Saxon King Ethelbert, and early bishops included St Paulinus and the first Anglo-Saxon bishop, Ithamar.

At the Dissolution, the priory was the last monastic house to submit to the Royal Commissioners, and Henry VIII, having appropriated the priory buildings as a royal palace, appointed the last prior as the first Dean of the cathedral.

The Civil War also took a heavy toll on the cathedral, with Col Sanders's parliamentarian troops plundering the cathedral, using the main part as a carpenter's shop. The eighteenth century saw construction of houses within the precincts, settings often used in the novels of Charles Dickens, and following further restorations by the Victorian architect Sir George Gilbert Scott, the cathedral has for the last century or so enjoyed a welcome period of tranquillity.

well as rabbits and guinea pigs, there were also orphan lambs, goats, turkeys and chickens. But only a few guinea pigs, rabbits, Felix, and Cleo the snake came to Rochester. One can't help but see Jonathan Meyrick as a sort of David Attenborough of cathedral life.

There is a certain lack of convention in the handing out of names to the family animals, however, so that Felix is not a cat, but a springer spaniel, though the poor chap does seem to suffer from some confusion about his species, swinging from barking at shadows, like any proper dog, to chasing birds and attempting to climb trees. Into this happy melange came Figaro, picked out by daughter Anastasia at a local cat rescue centre (with only eleven animals in the household Anastasia had been feeling understandably bereft).

Figaro is a handsome cheerful fellow, more like his counterpart in Mozart's opera than the kitty in Pinnochio, after whom he was actually named. Figaro took very little time to assert himself, ensuring that Felix the spaniel complied with his domestic needs, the most pressing of which was the use of Felix as a pillow. The Deanery garden became a favourite spot, from which Figaro could hop over into the High Street for the occasional excursion into the city centre. And he soon discovered the cloister garth, and the ruined walls of the chapter house. But the King's Garden became his regular haunt, much to the horror of the gardener's dog, who became so nervous that he flinched every time a leaf blew across the lawn.

Tower of London and the nearby Rochester Castle: clearly a man who intended his buildings to last! There are still some traces of original Roman brickwork in the nearby city walls, and notably in the footings of the walls of the ruined Chapter House, a favourite vantage point of Figaro, the Rochester Cathedral cat. Figaro has a superb territory, taking in the King's Gardens, the cloister garth (cathedral gardens) and the Deanery garden, as well as the elegance of nearby Minor Canon Row, and straying into the Dickensian cobbled lanes that criss-cross the nearby High Street. Canon Jonathan Meyrick – Acting Dean of the cathedral – and his family came to Rochester from a rural parish in Wiltshire, where animals were a dominant feature of domestic life. As

Squirrels packed their bags and left, birds declared a no-fly zone, and wildlife in general lived at red alert.

Back at home there was a shock in store. In Jonathan Meyrick's study there is a large heated glass tank, with a secure cover that Figaro likes to perch on. He wasn't much interested in the contents, just some greenery, sand and old pieces of wood. Then one day, he saw something move – or slither, rather – under a piece of wood. Alerted, Figaro hopped down and sat, nose pressed to the glass, waiting for further signs of movement. He sat and waited patiently, as only cats can do. After about half an hour he began to lose interest; he looked around, had a bit of a wash, and turned back to the glass tank, whereupon he found, gazing at him intently, a large snake. Figaro's life flashed before his eyes. Fur on end, he hurtled up the curtains, and there remained for quite a while.

From that point on, Figaro was reformed. He made a point of befriending the gardener's dog, and welcomed back into the cathedral gardens all the wild life that had previously moved out. There are still some unresolved issues with the other local cats – Figaro's relations with them are uneasy, being confined to invective hurled over his shoulder as he passes by. He has eventually become accustomed to Cleo, and sits outside her snake house, extending a (very) tentative paw to pat the glass if she emerges from hiding.

Figaro roams still, king of the night atop the ruined chapter house walls, silhouetted against a dusky sky. Maybe his nocturnal prowlings bring him face to face with the spirits of Dickens characters drifting through the darkened alleyways surrounding the cathedral – the enigmatic Mr Datchery, the Reverend Septimus Crisparkle with his 'china shepherdess mother' and the opium addict choirmaster John Jasper.

PREVIOUS PAGE
Cat, camouflaged
OPPOSITE LEFT
There are still some unresolved issues with local cats
ABOVE
Figaro, recovering from meeting Cleo, the snake

Wolfie
Salisbury Cathedral

'Of all God's creatures, there is only one that cannot be made slave of the leash. That one is the cat. If man could be crossed with the cat it would improve the man, but it would deteriorate the cat'

Mark Twain

Salisbury Cathedral takes its cats seriously. As well as Simkin, who featured in the first Cathedral Cats book, there was Captain, the Salisbury's first cathedral cat, and then Baggins, Ginger, Psyche, Tiddler and Sultan. The present Bishop of Salisbury has a cat called Topsy, and it is quite normal for a cat to take part in a cathedral procession – the traditional order being altar boy, verger, bishop, cat.

Celebrated in paintings by Joseph Turner and John Constable, Salisbury Cathedral is one of the most recognisable buildings in Britain, a unique example of unified Early English architecture. Built on foundations of no more than one and a half meters, and situated on a water meadow, Salisbury Cathedral

THE CATHEDRAL

Salisbury Cathedral is a unique example of unified Early English architecture. Built on foundations of no more than one and a half metres, on a water meadow, the cathedral has the tallest spire in Britain, and took just 38 years to complete. The octagonal spire was added about a hundred years after the first stone was laid, and has remained secure despite a pronounced lean at the top.

The cathedral interior vividly conveys the sense of vast space and austere grandeur of Early English architecture, in part due to the 'restoration work' of James Wyatt, which principally comprised the removal of medieval stained glass, the demolition of the Bell Tower, and the levelling of the churchyard. One of the treasures of the cathedral which he didn't get rid of is an ancient clock mechanism dating from 1386 and said to be the oldest piece of machinery still at work in Britain, if not the entire world.

Anthony Trollope set many of his novels in and around the cathedral, notably *The Warden* and *Barchester Towers*.

took just thirty-eight years to complete. The octagonal spire (the tallest in Britain) was added about a hundred years after the first stone was laid, and credit is due to the builders who spotted that the supporting piers were bending under the additional weight of material, and reinforced them with hundreds of tons of new material.

The extent of the residential close perhaps explains the proliferation of cats here. Wolfie first came to the cathedral as a kitten, and lived with Canon June Osborne, who had recently been appointed Dean of Salisbury Cathedral. After six months of perfectly happy home life, Wolfie inexplicably turned his back on a caring household. Some cats are naturally nomadic, and my guess is that he couldn't resist the

allure of the cathedral, with its wide-open spaces and friendly population. (To this day, though, the Dean remains Wolfie's official kin, paying for his veterinary care and upkeep, lucky cat.)

But it was not in Wolfie's stars to be a stray: he put in regular appearances in the cloisters, which the cathedral somehow acquired in the middle of the 13th century, despite never having been a monastic establishment. Their tranquillity belies the existence behind them of an extremely busy and industrious cathedral works department. And here Wolfie hung his hat, so to speak. The craftsmen of the works department have a well-established interest in cats; Ginger, now immortalized in a stained glass window depicting the laying of the original foundation stone

PREVIOUS PAGE
Wolfie casts a critical eye over the stonemasons' work
RIGHT
The cloisters, one of Wolfie's many cathedral haunts
OPPOSITE RIGHT
Waiting for Steve Mellor and Sunday roast chicken

of the cathedral, was a stoneyard resident. Wolfie took up residence, and for a while was looked after by the cathedral glaziers, whom he would follow up scaffolding and ladders, looking for all the world like a furry black gargoyle come to life. Wolfie's peripatetic habits brought him into contact with all walks of life. Cathedral publications manager Catherine Spender's daughter returned from her first day at the cathedral school, complaining of a black cat who sat on her lap throughout the Latin class. Soon after, Wolfie showed up at the visitor services desk, and so captivated the staff that he was provided with his own chair and a container of cat treats.

Not content with adopting the precincts, cloisters and workshops, Wolfie has also colonised the cathedral itself, slipping into the south aisle from the cloisters, or wailing pitifully by the south transept door until let in by a visitor. Fortunately for Wolfie, the tolerance threshold for cats is particularly high at Salisbury. Suzanne Edwards, the cathedral librarian, has carefully chronicled the lives of several of the cathedral cats, and Wolfie's signature appears frequently in the library visitors' book. Wolfie once turned up to an early morning Eucharist, where he sat by the server's chair on the right of the celebrant, gazing at the Dean. Then when the Dean went up to read the Gospel, Wolfie went too, sitting by the Dean while he read. Wolfie certainly enjoys the efforts that are made for his comfort: the Christmas crib, with its bed of straw and thatched shelter, makes an inviting bed, and visitors

are startled by the sight of a bleary-eyed Wolfie emerging from the serenity of the Christmas scene. During one Christingle (Christmas crib) service, Wolfie woke from a deep sleep to find himself the subject of a donkey's curious scrutiny. Having been cared for initially by the glaziers, Wolfie came into contact with Steve Mellor, of the works department, who took on the everyday care of Wolfie, feeding him and offering general companionship. Steve now feeds Wolfie every day of the year, with roast chicken for Sunday lunch, and he doesn't take holidays anymore, as he'd rather be with Wolfie. And what does Steve get in return? Well, as the author William S. Burroughs put it: 'The cat does not offer services. The cat offers itself. Of course he wants care and shelter. You don't buy love for nothing. Like all pure creatures, cats are practical.'

Jasper and Eddie
Southwell Minster

*'Cats are smarter than dogs. You can't get
eight cats to pull a sled through snow'*
Jeff Valdez

The cathedral cats of Southwell Minster live with
Richard Davey, Residentiary Canon, his wife Sam and
their daughter Caitlin. The Daveys previously spent
four years at St Edmundsbury, where Richard would
walk around the churchyard with their black and white
cat Sylvester, fending off the not entirely well-
intentioned advances of Daisy and Lazarus (see St
Edmundsbury Cathedral). It is curious that, in such a
large area, all the cathedral cats of St Edmundsbury
should decide that they all need to be in the same spot
at the same time. When Jasper, a little white kitten
from a cat rescue centre, was added to the Davey
menagerie, there was widespread outrage – but all the
wailing and squawking had no effect on Jasper, since
he is stone deaf. Jasper's initial outings were secular:

THE CATHEDRAL

Set in a sleepy market town, Southwell Minster nestles
comfortably into its semi-rural surroundings, modestly signalling
its existence with two distinctive 'pepperpot' spires. The Saxon
Minster church was established by Oskytel, Archbishop of York,
towards the latter part of the eighth century. Remains of the tile
floor can still be seen, as well as a lintel over a doorway in the
North transept, depicting St Michael battling the dragon, and
David with the lion and lamb.

This was replaced with a Norman structure, and then, towards
the end of the 1200s, Southwell acquired another of its
architectural treasures, the Chapter House. This architectural and
historical gem was originally decorated in vivid colours: it is a riot
of carvings, depicting animals, plants, trees and fruits, all of which
probably served as a very early form of visual aid to a largely
illiterate congregation. In 1884, the Minster acquired its present
status as cathedral for the newly created Southwell diocese.

PREVIOUS PAGE
A deaf Jasper and an earth-bound
Eddie
BELOW
Although deaf, Jasper tracks the dogs
through vibration
OPPOSITE RIGHT
Eddie reflects on the problems of

he had a favourite pub close to the cathedral, and started to show signs of wanting to visit the nearby brewery. This meant crossing a busy road, dangerous at the best of times, but for a deaf cat potentially lethal, so a protesting Jasper was confined to quarters. As for Sylvester, whenever the Daveys went away he would disappear, only reappearing after the Daveys had got to the point of putting up 'missing' posters – at which point he'd stroll in as though nothing had happened. Perhaps that was why the Daveys were relieved to move to Southwell Minster, a peaceful contrast to the bustle of Bury St Edmunds. Cathedrals are often described as 'magnificent' or 'imposing', but here the term 'enchanting' springs to mind more readily. Southwell Minster nestles comfortably into its semi-rural surroundings, modestly signalling its existence with two 'pepperpot' spires. At the east end of the cathedral is an open-ended quadrangle of Georgian houses, and this is where Jasper and Sylvester were safely installed (once Jasper had been persuaded to stop playing with leaves in the middle of the road).

Their newfound peace did not last long: the arrival of Max, Fen and Hal, collie, lurcher and whippet puppies respectively, ensured that Jasper and Sylvester were kept on their paws. The three dogs did nothing but rush around the house, gobbling up the cat food, barging into rooms uninvited and crashing into tables. Without hearing, Jasper was nonetheless able to tell the whereabouts of the dogs in the house from the vibrations of wagging tails beating against doors and walls, and the scrabbling of paws on the wooden and stone floors. While Jasper tracked them, Sylvester nosed the dogs' food dishes into a narrow space by the washing machine. With the dogs sugbjugated, Sylvester was free to settle into semi-retirement, by which time another cat had arrived – Eddie. Eddie too considered himself to be vastly superior to the three dogs: he could never understand why they always looked so anxious, especially when by the washing machine.

As Sylvester grew older, Eddie took over the more active of his responsibilities, and when Sylvester died, Eddie was given his collar, confirming his seniority in the animal hierarchy of the household. To tell the truth, he wasn't very good at it, disappearing for up to a week at a time, and getting involved in some rather questionable adventures. In short, Eddie lived up to his name – which he had taken from Eddie the Eagle, an amiable but catastrophic ski-jumper. Eddie the cat seemed determined to emulate his namesake's spectacular but misjudged airborne antics. One evening, having climbed a tree to get a better vantage point over an outdoor concert at the cathedral, Eddie got so carried away that he launched himself from the top of the tree into thin air. To his surprise, flapping his paws didn't really work, and he landed in a spread-eagled pile beside a startled verger. Learning from experience isn't one of Eddie's strong points: he persisted in his flight experiments, undeterred even by a bad landing on ice which broke his pelvis. Eddie was

kept in a cage to ensure that he kept still enough for the break to heal, but he escaped, and persuaded Max the Collie to provide some motive power for another flight attempt. Eddie would sit on the first floor window ledge of the Davey's house, while Max took a nose-first run at him from the other side of the room. It certainly got Eddie started, and he managed about five feet in the horizontal flight before gravity took over and he landed in a heap on the grass below. Both he and Jasper have great fun scratching marks into the trees that line the Minster churchyard, a type of feline mason's mark that echoes the marks of the original stone masons that are scattered throughout Southwell Minster.

Adam and Florence
Westminster Abbey

'If animals could speak the dog would be a blundering outspoken fellow, but the cat would have the rare grace of never saying a word too much'

Mark Twain

Although Westminster Abbey is not a cathedral, this 'House of Kings' has a unique place in the history of Britain, and it was from here that the inspiration came for the original *Cathedral Cats*. Biggles, the Abbey caterers' cat, was the hero of that tale, now living in sedate retirement on a farm. There were then, as now, many other cats living at the abbey, and a fair few who just pass through. Many of these make their way through the home ground of Adam and Florence, who live with the Very Rev. Canon David Hutt in a secluded Georgian house overlooking the College garden.

When David Hutt set out one morning to prepare two sisters for confirmation, he didn't know that he was about to experience a moment of great personal

THE CATHEDRAL

Despite being in the heart of London, Westminster Abbey manages to keep its distance from the noise, rush and swirl of urban life. The Abbey itself may be crowded with tourists, but in the South Cloisters, or sitting in the Abbey Gardens, peace can be found.

Edward the Confessor, the last of the Anglo-Saxon kings, built the original Benedictine Abbey at Westminster. By the 12th century, the Abbey had become a thriving centre of pilgrimage to his tomb, with the monastic community caring for the pilgrims and tending the College Garden, probably the oldest in England.

Westminster Abbey is neither a cathedral nor a parish church. When Elizabeth I refounded the abbey, the original monastic community was replaced by a dean and chapter, and in 1560 was constituted as a 'Royal Peculiar', accountable only to the Sovereign. There are monarchs, politicians, warriors, scientists, musicians and poets all buried here.

change too. During the morning conversations and discussions, his eyes were continually drawn to two Burmese cats, who were clearly most interested in him. When the pastoral aspect of the morning drew to a close, the conversation turned to cats. David, with no direct experience of cats, remarked upon the fine appearance and character of the Burmese cats, who by this time had decided to settle by him. The conversation turned in due course to the work of cat rescue centres; before he quite realised what was happening, David was at the local centre, being

introduced to three cats, Adam and Eve, a pair of discarded Christmas kittens, and Florence, who had been rescued separately from the city streets. While at the centre Adam and Florence had formed an affinity, and David Hutt decided to take them. Two more appreciative cats it would have been difficult to find. They took to vicarage life with gusto, exploring every nook and cranny, and displaying a touching devotion to their saviour. Adam showed so much interest in the various meetings at the vicarage that he was given his own chair: he would sit on it, chin resting on the table before him, giving the appearance of following every word uttered, while Florence would sit patiently underneath Adam's chair. Then came the move to Westminster Abbey, and a second chance to observe London life from inside a car. Florence was a bit queasy, but Adam showed all the signs of becoming a wannabe driver, impatiently tapping his paws whilst waiting for the green light. At last they came through the south cloisters, down an enclosed stone passage way, into the College Garden, and so to their new home, a wisteria-shaded Georgian house.

By the twelfth century, the Abbey at Westminster had become a thriving centre of pilgrimage to the tomb of Edward the Confessor, with the monastic community dividing their duties between prayer, maintenance of the Abbey and caring for the pilgrims. The well-tended College Garden, probably the oldest in England, has been looked after continuously for over 900 years. Originally a source of medicinal herbs, as well as a source of food, apples, pears and even vines were cultivated. Hyssop and fennel still grow here, much to the interest of the cats, who frequently stand by the fennel, noses raised and eyes shut. The garden is now used for special events, and has recently been opened to the public, and Adam and Florence have exploited this to the full – David has been sent photographs of the cats in the garden by captivated visitors from all over the world. Adam did once manage to climb one of the trees, but getting down was another thing altogether, and the gardeners embarked on a rescue mission. Better scrambling areas are provided by the fourteenth century stone precinct walls that bound part of the garden.

Summer is a time for visiting neighbours: both cats set out quite early, exchanging relatively polite greetings with Denis, the verger's cat who lives nearby. In fact Denis is usually on his way to David Hutt's house for a second breakfast, while Florence, with the same object in mind, is making for Denis's residence. Adam normally makes do with only the one meal to start his day, and then strolls over to the cloisters, and thence to Dean's Yard, where he passes the time of day with visitors and abbey staff – if only he could pick up David's mail for him! Adam is a water and ice cat: he'll sit for hours by the pool in the Little Cloister, watching the water from the central fountain falling back, taking an occasional drink, every now and again dipping a paw. At home the sounds of running water, or of tinkling ice in a glass always bring him running;

when the fridge is defrosted he hooks out some of the ice, and whacks it like a hockey puck around the house. He gets a bit confused when the ice melts, but then we can't all be scientists. This fascination for ice draws Adam to any cocktail party going. That and olives, which both cats go for in a big way.

Then there are various fund-raising and special events that take place in the garden. As a 'Royal Peculiar' the Abbey is accountable only to the Sovereign, and is the setting for a variety of glittering events. All coronations since 1066 – save two – have taken place here, and numerous other royal and state occasions as well. Life is put into perspective when one sees, among the splendour of ceremonial uniforms, ecclesiastical regalia and extravagant garden party hats, Adam and Florence, two most ordinary cats wandering around, perfectly at home with the great and the good.

Marmaduke, Fatcat and PJ
Worcester Cathedral

'Cats are intended to teach us that not everything in nature has a purpose'
Garrison Keillor

Worcester Cathedral has been a place of pilgrimage since the death and canonisation of Oswald, founder of the Benedictine community at Worcester. The cathedral is set in an idyllic position on the banks of the River Severn, where it has become an accidental icon for that most English of pastimes, cricket! After Bishop Wulfstan's canonization, the cathedral became an ever more popular centre of pilgrimage, and King John was buried within it.

The increasing revenues that pilgrimages brought to the cathedral allowed for steady progress in restoration and development, culminating in a great rededication in the presence of Henry III in 1218. By the beginning of the fifteenth century, Worcester

THE CATHEDRAL

Worcester Cathedral's magnificent architecture and rich history make it an oasis of beauty among the concrete jungle of city centre shops thrown up in the 1960s. It was also the site, in 1717, of the first Three Choirs Festival, which continues to this day in worldwide renown.

The second cathedral here was built by Oswald, whose canonisation increased its importance, but it was on the canonisation of Wulfstan, who built the third cathedral, that it really began to draw in the pilgrims, so that it became an important enough place for King John to be buried here.

Inside today's cathedral can be found a plaque commemorating 'Woodbine Willy', a battlefront chaplain during the Great War who handed out copies of the New Testament together with packs of cigarettes. A more famous son of Worcester is the composer Sir Edward Elgar, remembered in the magnificent 'Gerontius' stained-glass window close to the north door.

Cathedral was much as it is today. The cathedral is still surrounded by small remnants of the Benedictine monastery, which combine with the remains of the cloister and the walled gardens to create a quadrangle giving the cathedral close, or College Green, as it is now known, the intimate air of an Oxford college.

Marmaduke, a portly and genial ginger cat, lives in a secluded corner of College Green with the cathedral organist Adrian Lucas, his wife Joanna and their children Hannah and William. He is one of a long line of rescue cats taken in by the Lucas family over the years. The household is a highly musical one, with a steady flow of students taking lessons, as well as Adrian's own musical activities and preparations. There are the childrens'musical activities too, notably William Lucas's trombone practice. This is something that Marmaduke doesn't care to listen to much; he pleads urgent business elsewhere. On one occasion Marmaduke was in such a hurry to get out of earshot that he scampered up the steps into College Hall (originally the monastery refectory) to find himself in the midst of some eighty students just starting a Maths A-level exam. Spying an empty chair, he sat down quietly, trying to avoid the eagle-eyed invigilators; but, alas, he was spotted, and being unable to produce his candidate number, was politely but firmly escorted out.

Music is impossible to avoid at Worcester Cathedral, which was the site, in 1717, of the first Three Choirs Festival, an event which has become world-famous; to this day the cathedral choir maintains a great English choral tradition, and is listened to throughout the world. The composer Sir Edward Elgar, celebrated son of Worcester, is remembered in the magnificent 'Gerontius' stained-glass window close to the north door. So for music-eschewing Marmaduke the rule is: never go near the cathedral during the festival (concerts) or in the late afternoon (evensong), on Sunday mornings, or on any of the other days (and there are many) when there are recitals or other

PREVIOUS PAGE
PJ, watched over by Fate

RIGHT
The amiable Marmaduke beams a welcome

OPPOSITE LEFT
Fat Cat, who really wants to be a duck

capable of showing irritation too. When the Lucases come back from a weekend away, or from holiday, Marmaduke is usually sitting in the hall waiting, not to show his delight at their return but to bestow an irritable nip on the first ankle he can get to as the family come through the door. There is therefore a strict rota for who goes in first on these occasions! The Lucases recently took in two new rescue cats, Wulstan and Oswald, who are even less keen on music than Marmaduke, but tend to make the rather unwise choice of hiding inside the grand piano: Adrian has found that the only way of dislodging them is to play Lizst.

Meanwhile, at the other end of the college green, by the medieval gatehouse that leads into College Green, live Canon Alvyn Pettersen and his family. They came to Worcester from Frensham, where daughter Catherine busied herself creating a miniature farm (she describes herself as a 'farmer in the making'). It would have been too much for Catherine to leave behind all her animals, so most of them came with her: the Pettersen's cathedral house garden is a cheerful melange of ducks, dogs, cats and chickens. Canon Pettersen drew the line at the pig and goats, and the sheep are at a nearby farm. Consequently, although spared the bleating of sheep, the peace of College Green is sometimes disturbed by barking, clucking, quacking, the hoarse call of a harassed rooster, and the occasional meow from a cat called, perhaps somewhat unkindly, FatCat. FatCat is another

concerts. In order to keep himself music-free, Marmaduke generally confines his cathedralic appearances to the cloisters and the gift shop, a haven of warmth when the cold wind sweeps off the river, and College Green.

Marmaduke is a cat of transparent emotions: to see him sitting and waiting for Joanna Lucas to come home from work is a touching experience. When he spies her coming through the medieval gate-house, he sits and smiles! If that beaming smile could be captured and suspended in a tree, one would have the perfect Cheshire Cat. But Marmaduke is more than rescue cat, and has to bear the indignity of being named differently by each member of the family – she is known variously as FatCat, Pirelli, Humbug and Schmuck, but the variation doesn't matter as all of these names is equally useless in getting her attention. With the menagerie of animals around, FatCat suffers to a significant degree from an inferiority complex. Her instincts are to chase the ducks and chickens, but they are all bigger, and chase her. So rather than be excluded for bad behaviour, she tries to join in, although she does draw the line at the duck pond. FatCat's style is also cramped by Jumbo, an affable collie, who insists on following her around. Imagine how irritating it must be when you've just settled down under a bush for a bit of ornithology, when a breathless and excited dog crashes through the undergrowth, asking if he can play too!

Dogs figure in the lives of other cats around the cathedral too. Down by the riverside, in an old Victorian cottage and boathouse, lives Steve Smith, the cathedral Services Manager, with his wife Marcelle and their daughter Sian. This is another household where devotion to animals is apparent everywhere, but cats are clearly the heroes here. The house has been home to several pure-bred cats: Cleo and Nero, two Bengal cats, elegantly adorned the riverside gardens, until one day they were stolen. They were replaced by an Abyssinian female, from whom Sian hoped to breed. The neighbourhood tomcats helped out. The family knew who the culprits were, and were thinking of

suing for maintenance. So now the house has PJ, a mild-mannered and polite mostly-Abyssinian, who likes to sit at the foot of the steps leading up to the family's house. He's a real young gent, and completes the circle of cats that surround Worcester Cathedral. Sian is not too worried about PJ being taken from the public gardens, as he is watched over by a beady-eyed, stocky bull-terrier who is rather aptly named Fate.

OPPOSITE LEFT
A 'young gent' of a cat
BELOW
Markaduke waits for trombone practice to finish

Acknowledgements

St Edmundsbury Cathedral, Bury St Edmunds – *Lazarus & Daisy* Canon Andrew and the Rev. Catherine Todd

Canterbury Cathedral – *Magic* Canon Richard and Mrs Elizabeth Marsh, Phoebe Marsh; *Rhubarb & Fungus* Canon Edward and Mrs Sarah Condry

Chelmsford Cathedral – *Tomkins* Mr Peter Nardone

Chester Cathedral – *Olsen & Hansen* the Rt Rev. Dr Peter Forster, Bishop of Chester

Chichester Cathedral – *Claude & Bookie* the Rev. Nicholas and Mrs Marieke Biddle

Durham Cathedral – *Leofric & Godiva* the Very Rev. Michael and Mrs Jennifer Sadgrove

St Mary's Episcopal Cathedral, Edinburgh – *Cassiopeia & Wallace* the Rev. William Mountsey, the Rev. Dean Fosterkew; *Winston* Canon Jane Millard, Vice Provost

Ely Cathedral – *Hamish* Mr Martin and Mrs Paula Fleet; *Harry & Boots* Mr Stephen and Mrs Stefanie Wikner; *Dilly, Suajeta & Scheherazade* the Porter-Thaw family

Exeter Cathedral – *Emma & Thomas* Canon Neil Collins

Gloucester Cathedral – *Bonnie & Flora* Canon David Hoyle

Hereford Cathedral – *Saffron & Mevagissey* Mr Peter Dyke and Mr Shaun Ward. Hereford Cathedral photograph by D. Harbour, reproduced by kind permission of the Dean and Chapter of Hereford Cathedral

Lichfield Cathedral – *Kim & Boris* Mr Mark Jervis

Portsmouth Cathedral – *Ivor* Mr David and Mrs Kitty Price

Ripon Cathedral – *Samson & Delilah* the Very Rev. John and Mrs Bridgit Methuen

Rochester Cathedral – *Figaro* Canon Jonathan and Mrs Rebecca Meyrick

Salisbury Cathedral – *Wolfie* the Very Rev. June Osborne, Mr Steve Mellor

Southwell Minster – *Jasper & Eddie* Canon Richard and Mrs Samantha Holgate Davey

Westminster Abbey – *Adam & Flora* Canon David Hutt

Worcester Cathedral – *Marmaduke* Adrian and Joanna Lucas; *FatCat* Canon Alvyn and Mrs Judith Pettersen, Catherine Pettersen; *PJ* Sian Smith